W9-AAV-801

Indigenous Peoples of the World

The
Amazon

Anne Wallace Sharp

LUCENT BOOKS®

THOMSON

GALE

San Diego • Detroit • New York • San Francisco • Cleveland • New Haven, Conn. • Waterville, Maine • London • Munich

THOMSON

✳ ™

GALE

3 1969 01416 9790

LIBRARY OF CONGRESS CATALOGING-IN-PUBLICATION DATA

Sharp, Anne Wallace.
   The Amazon / by Anne Wallace Sharp.
      p. cm. — (Indigenous peoples of the world)
  Summary: Discusses the historical origins, beliefs, arts, family life, cultural clashes with
whites, and future hopes of the Amerindians of the Amazon.
  Includes bibliographical references and index.
    ISBN 1-59018-313-4 (hardback : alk. paper)
    1. Indians of South America—Amazon River Region—History—Juvenile literature.
2. Indians of South America—Amazon River Region—Social America—Amazon River
Region.] I. Title. II. Indigenous peoples of the world (San Diego, Calif.)
    F2519.1.A6S55 2004
    981'.100498—dc21

          2003011136

Printed in the United States of America

Contents

Foreword

Nearly every area of the world has indigenous populations, those people who are descended from the original settlers of a given region, often arriving many millennia ago. Many of these populations exist today despite overwhelming odds against their continuing survival.

Though indigenous populations have come under attack for a variety of reasons, in most cases, land lies at the heart of the conflict. The hunger for land has threatened indigenous societies throughout history, whether the aggressor was a neighboring tribe or a foreign culture. The reason for this is simple: For indigenous populations, *way of life* has nearly always depended on the land and its bounty. Indeed, cultures from the Inuit of the frigid Arctic to the Yanomami of the torrid Amazon rain forest have been indelibly shaped by the climate and geography of the regions they inhabit.

As newcomers moved into already settled areas of the world, competition led to tension and violence. When newcomers possessed some important advantages—greater numbers or more powerful weapons—the results were predictable. History is rife with examples of outsiders triumphing over indigenous populations. Anglo-Saxons and Vikings, for instance, moved into eastern Europe and the British Isles at the expense of the indigenous Celts. Europeans traveled south through Africa and into Australia displacing the indigenous Bushmen and Aborigines, while other Westerners ventured into the Pacific at the expense of the indigenous Melanesians, Micronesians, and Polynesians. In North and South America, the colonization of the New World by European powers resulted in the decimation and displacement of numerous Native American groups.

Nevertheless, many indigenous populations retained their identity and managed to survive. Only in the last one hundred years, however, have anthropologists begun to study, with any objectivity, the hundreds of indigenous societies found throughout the world. Only within the last few decades have these societies been truly appreciated and acknowledged for their richness and complexity. The ability to adapt to and manage their environments is but one marker of the incredible resourcefulness of many indigenous populations. The Inuit, for example, created two, distinct modes of travel for getting around the barren, icy region that is their home. The sleek, speedy kayak—with its whalebone frame and sealskin cover—allowed the Inuit to silently skim the waters of the nearby ocean and bays. The sledge (or dogsled)—with its caribou-hide platform and runners built from whalebone or frozen fish covered with sealskin —made travel over the snow- and ice-covered landscape possible.

The Indigenous Peoples of the World series strives to present a clear and realistic picture of the world's many and varied native cultures. The series captures the uniqueness as well as the similarities of indigenous societies by examining family and community life, traditional spirituality and religion, warfare, adaptation to the environment, and interaction with other native and nonnative peoples.

The series also offers perspective on the effects of Western civilization on indigenous populations, as well as a multifaceted view of contemporary life. Many indigenous societies, for instance, struggle today with poverty, unemployment, racism, poor health, and a lack of educational opportunities. Others find themselves embroiled in political instability, civil unrest, and violence. Despite the problems facing these societies, many indigenous populations have regained a sense of pride in themselves and their heritages. Many have also experienced a resurgence of traditional art and culture as they seek to find a place for themselves in the modern world.

The Indigenous Peoples of the World series offers an in-depth study of different regions of the world and the people who have long inhabited those regions. All books in the series include fully documented, primary and secondary source quotations that enliven the text. Sidebars highlight notable events, personalities, and traditions, while annotated bibliographies offer ideas for future research. Numerous maps and photographs provide the reader with a pictorial glimpse of each society.

From the Aborigines of Australia to the various indigenous peoples of the Caribbean, Europe, South America, Mexico, Asia, and Africa, the series covers a multitude of societies and their cultures. Each book stands alone, and the series as a collection offers valuable comparisons of the past history and future problems of the indigenous peoples of the world.

The Amazon and Its Inhabitants

For hundreds of years, the Amazon basin of South America has fascinated, mystified, and attracted explorers and adventurers. Impenetrable jungles, towering trees, mighty rivers, and exotic animals await those who venture into this vast area. Many who have entered the region have described the area in glowing terms; others have left derogatory, darker accounts. "The pessimists," writes historian Marshall C. Eakin, "see nothing but dense jungle, unbearable heat and humidity, hundreds of deadly predators, and tropical disease."[1] Other descriptions tell stories of gold, lost cities, warlike indigenous people, and unusual plants and animals, all of which have given the Amazon its reputation as a region of mystery and wonder.

The Amazon

The Amazon River, called the River-Sea by early explorers, was born many millions of years ago when a vast inland sea burst its shores and began an eastward journey across the continent of South America. Today hundreds of small streams join larger tributaries that swell and flow toward the east till they join the major body of water called the Amazon River—by volume, the largest river in the world. Four thousand miles long, the Amazon empties into the Atlantic Ocean in northern Brazil.

The rivers and streams are surrounded by millions of acres of rain forest—dense canopy, jungles, and lush undergrowth—more than 80 percent of which is undeveloped. The area is so dense and difficult to penetrate, in fact, that many thousands of square miles have never been explored.

The rivers and rain forests of the Amazon basin, covering nearly half of South America, compose an area called Amazonia, which encompasses the greater part of Brazil and parts of eight other countries: Peru, Ecuador, Bolivia, Venezuela, Surinam, French Guiana, Guyana, and Colombia. Photojournalist Loren McIntyre sums up his impressions of the region: "One is struck by Amazonia's capacity to astonish."[2]

The Indigenous People of the Amazon

The first settlers to the Americas came from Asia and crossed the Bering Strait into Alaska nearly twenty thousand years ago. Living by hunting and gathering, these travelers moved southward in search of food over many thousands of years. Some settled in North America, while others moved into Mexico, and still others continued their migration into South America. Anthropologists believe that the Amazon basin was settled around ten thousand years ago, and estimate by between 6 million and 9 million Amerindians inhabited the region 1500 B.C.

By that time, many of these early people had given up their nomadic ways of life and begun a more settled existence. Scat-

tered tribes began to grow their own food instead of gathering it, cultivating corn and other vegetables. Numerous small farming and fishing communities grew up along the rivers, and, in time, each developed unique traditions and ways of life, many of which are still practiced today. Other groups of Amerindians chose to continue their hunting and gathering traditions and made semipermanent homes deeper in the forests and jungles of the Amazon.

The Amazon Today

After their initial contact with Europeans at the beginning of the sixteenth century, indigenous populations declined rapidly, a decline that continued throughout the twentieth century. No one knows for sure how many Amerindians live in the Amazon basin today. Although estimates range up

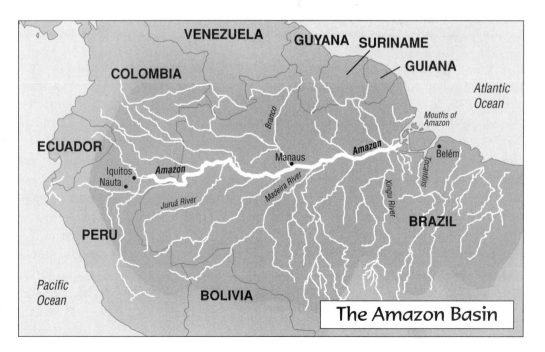

The Amazon Basin

☀ Facts About the Amazon

Over the last several hundred years, historians and scientists have written some amazing facts about the Amazon. Words such as *biggest, largest, best, most,* and other superlatives are often used to describe the area.

The Amazon River, for instance, is the deepest river in the world, reaching a depth of over 250 feet in several places. While not the longest river (the Nile River holds that status), it is the second longest and holds the distinction of being the largest river in terms of water volume. Scientists claim that the Amazon contains more water than the Nile and Mississippi Rivers combined. One day's worth of water from the mouth of the Amazon could supply all the homes in the United States with enough water to last five months. No bridge spans the Amazon River anywhere along its route. In fact, in some areas, the Amazon is over two hundred miles wide.

The Amazon basin is a treasure trove of plants and animals. More varieties of life are found here than anywhere else on Earth. More than 30 million species of insects, for instance, make their homes in the Amazon. In addition, more than fifteen hundred kinds of birds, three thousand different fish, and an estimated 5 million different plant species live in the region.

The Amazon basin is one of the wettest regions in the world, with an average rainfall of over one hundred inches a year.

to 1 million, most researchers agree that the Amerindian population is probably closer to 250,000.

This population comprises hundreds of different Amerindian groups of varying size and composition. A few of these groups have never seen anyone or anything from outside the jungle, while hundreds of others are struggling to survive and adapt to contact with the modern world while retaining their traditional ways of life.

The Amazon basin ecosystem has also undergone devastating changes since the mid–eighteenth century. The rapid destruction of the rain forests is the most alarming modern development, but pollution, oil drilling, and gold mining have also harmed the ecology of the region.

Despite these problems and others, there is hope for the future. The indigenous people, for the first time in their history, are demanding and sometimes getting a voice in the decisions that affect their ways of life. In addition, various environmental groups are bringing worldwide attention to the plight of the Amazon and its rain forests.

Chapter 1

Adapting to Life in the Amazon

When the various indigenous groups arrived in the Amazon thousands of years ago, they found a unique and challenging environment. The Amerindians soon discovered that the forests and rivers could provide everything they needed in order to survive. They found ample supplies of food; cooking and lighting oil; bark and fiber for clothing, shelter, baskets, and hammocks; and plants with a variety of medicinal properties. In addition, the abundant wildlife enabled the indigenous people to make wide use of the area for hunting and fishing.

As the various Amerindians settled into this new environment, they began to devise unique ways to utilize the Amazon's resources. Ethnobotanist Mark Plotkin describes this adaptation: "A Westerner looks at the jungle and sees green. An Indian looks at the jungle and sees a grocery, a hardware store, a repair shop, and a pharmacy."[3]

Transportation

Efficient means of transportation were among the most immediate needs of the in-digenous people of the Amazon, who could travel only by foot or by river. Land travel was further limited to what an individual could carry, so many Amerindians turned to waterborne transportation by canoe, enabling them to hunt, fish, and move from place to place relatively easily.

The Warao Amerindians, for instance, used two different kinds of canoe in their coastal Venezuelan homeland. The simpler version, built of bark and used primarily for fishing, held two or three people. The other model, laboriously formed from the trunk of a giant hardwood tree, served as both a war canoe in times of conflict and a vessel with room for an entire village on a journey to a new location. Historian Alvin M. Josephy Jr. describes the larger vessel as "a dugout canoe holding fifty or more people and capable of making long voyages."[4]

Most indigenous people utilized a communal labor system in which all the men took part in the construction of a big canoe. Such a project, which could take two to three years to complete, usually began early in the

Dwarfed by the rain forest, an Amazonian Indian guides a canoe down the Amazon River. Indigenous peoples have traveled by canoe for millennia.

The Amazon Rain Forest

The Amazon rain forest is the largest tropical rain forest remaining on Earth. One of the most complex ecosystems anywhere, the rain forest is composed of many different layers and components.

The canopy, or "roof of the forest," is formed by the tallest trees in the area, usually mahogany and brazilwood, which are sometimes over two hundred feet tall. The tops of these trees are extremely close together and, as a consequence, absorb most of the sunlight before it reaches the forest floor. The canopy is home to huge numbers of animals, primarily butterflies, birds, small monkeys, bats, squirrels, and small cats like the ocelot.

The understory forms the next level of the rain forest. This is a particularly dark and moist area, and is characterized by small trees and climbing plants called lianas that wrap themselves around the big tree trunks. Howler monkeys, jaguars, and sloths make their homes in this level. Since just 2 percent of available sunlight penetrates to the understory, over thousands of years, plants have evolved means of adapting to low light levels.

The final layer is the forest floor itself. Very little rainfall or sunlight reaches this nutrient-poor area, which is primarily inhabited by insects and fungi that feed on the dead leaves of the forest.

summer dry season. At that time, multiple cuts and slashes were made in the trunk of a large brazilwood, mahogany, or other hardwood tree. The tree was then left alone and allowed to die.

The following fall, when the rains began, craftsmen directed numerous small fires at the base of the tree. Others cut away the burned wood with a tool called an adze, an axlike implement made of large conch shells, until the tree fell. The huge trunk was then cut to the proper length for a canoe, usually around fifteen to twenty feet, and the work of scraping and chipping continued. When the last of the bark had been removed, the tree was floated down the river to the village.

Under the watchful eye of a master builder, the charring and scraping process was continued for a period of nearly a year, until the tree had been properly hollowed out. When the log was roughly in its final shape, it was widened by fire, water, and steam. The final result was a sturdy and beautiful canoe, and the men who built it were treated with great respect and considered to be supernaturally gifted.

Finding Shelter

The hot and rainy tropical Amazon climate necessitated building shelters that could keep the elements at bay. The homes constructed by the indigenous people of the Amazon varied from simple thatched-roof

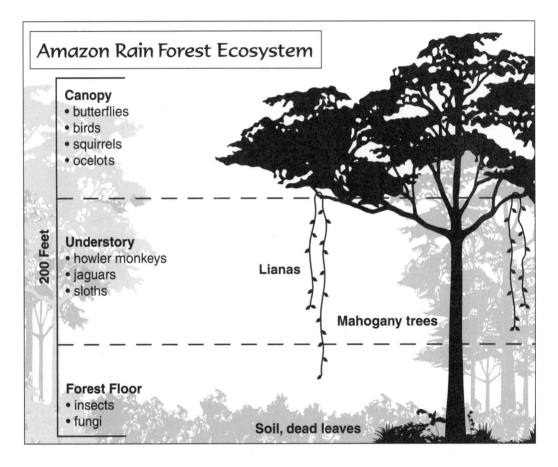

Amazon Rain Forest Ecosystem

Canopy
• butterflies
• birds
• squirrels
• ocelots

Understory
• howler monkeys
• jaguars
• sloths

200 Feet

Lianas

Mahogany trees

Forest Floor
• insects
• fungi

Soil, dead leaves

huts to large communal dwellings that could house as many as two hundred people. Many of these designs are still in use today.

When writer Carolyn Bennett Patterson visited the Txukahamei of Brazil, she stayed in a typical indigenous hut. Describing it, she writes, "Small, thatched, dirt-floored, the hut's only furnishing was a hammock strung from one side to the other."[5] Such one-room huts also featured open fire pits made of clay which were located in the middle of the floor; the rising smoke escaped from the hut through a hole in the roof. Some huts housed only a small family, while others were large

and roomy enough to provide a safe haven for an entire extended family.

The Jivaro of Ecuador and Peru lived in oval, wooden houses called *jivarias*, each of which was home to an extended family of up to forty people. These structures were built of heavy posts and beams that were held together with vines and then covered with palm thatch; they, too, featured a smoke hole in the roof.

Those Amerindian groups who lived along the rivers built their houses on stilts to accommodate seasonal flooding. The stilts also protected the indigenous people from forest rodents and insects. Some modern-day Amerindians leave their homes during the wet season and move to a floating house, while utilizing separate floating rafts for their livestock.

Communal Homes

The long house, or *maloca*, home to an entire community, was and remains the traditional dwelling of several Amerindian groups. *Malocas* generally had mud walls and thatched roofs. The families who were sheltered there slept in hammocks and gathered together for meals.

The Tucanoa chose to live in communal *malocas*. Their houses generally had two doorways. One entrance at the front of the house faced the river and was used exclusively by men. A rear door opened toward the jungle and was used by women and children. The house fires and kitchen areas were located toward the back of the house and were the domain of Tucanoan women and girls, who spent their time cleaning and cooking.

The Yanomami of Brazil and Venezuela called their large communal home a *shabono*. This disk-shaped structure featured an open-air, central-plaza courtyard. *Shabono* dwellings usually lasted only a year or two because the palm leaves in the roof quickly dried out and became infested with insects. When this occurred, the villagers burned the structure and built another.

This large structure is the communal home of a band of Yanomami Indians. Many Amazonian tribes live in such communal shelters.

The villages of the Kayapo of Brazil were arranged as a circle of houses with one or more large houses in the center. Families lived in the outer ring of homes, but only the men used the central house, which was a special place to gather socially and meet to make decisions that affected the entire village. The Mundurucu of Brazil also built special men's houses, where the warriors gathered to make their traditional bows and arrows and to recount the tribe's myths and stories.

The Wayana of French Guiana built their villages along the Maroni River. Each village featured a large communal hut used for special gatherings and ceremonies called a *tukusipan*. Circular in shape and covered with palm thatch, the *tukusipan*'s most distinctive feature was a large, wooden disk, or *maluana*, that had been cut from a cross section of the trunk of a fromager tree. The disk was painted with depictions of forest animals and played an important role in the Wayana belief system.

Clothing and Accessories

In the tropical climate of the Amazon, most of the indigenous people went barefoot and wore little, if any, clothing. Those who did wear clothes generally left their upper bodies bare, choosing to cover their lower bodies with various pieces made of palm, bark, or other natural material.

Wayana women, for instance, wore only a *weyu*, a kind of apron that left the buttocks exposed. Other indigenous women wore a short wraparound skirt, tied around the hips, called a *kamisa*. Penare men in western Guiana wore traditional loincloths, while the women clothed themselves in colored skirts of midcalf length.

Many Amerindians in the Peruvian jungles, on the other hand, wore clothing that covered a good portion of their bodies. These indigenous people lived in the shadow of the lofty Andes, where the climate tended to be cooler than the rest of the Amazon basin. As a result, many groups chose to wear a *kushma*, an item of clothing also used by the Inca of Peru. *Kushmas* were woven on a loom and made of natural, hand-spun cotton. The feather work that decorated the shoulders of these garments was worn exclusively by males and signified their skills at hunting and warfare.

Kayapo boys and girls of Brazil often wore variously, colored cloth bands tied, and sometimes crisscrossed, across their chests or tied together below their waists. The elders and chiefs in Kayapo society wore headdresses made of brightly, colored feathers. Most Amerindians in the Amazon, in fact, adorned themselves liberally with beautiful feather necklaces and earrings.

Body Paint and Decoration

Although they made little use of clothing, most of the indigenous people of the Amazon decorated their bodies with various kinds of paint and ornamentation. Body paint, for instance, represented an important part of Amerindian culture, as the various colors and designs were often used to tell the story of a group's or individual's history. Meant to be highly symbolic, body paint also helped deflect biting insects.

In preparation for a ceremony, an Amazon Indian applies body paint to another's face. Body paint designs reflect the status of the people bearing them.

Red and black were the primary colors used by the indigenous groups. The Yanomami, for instance, used a black dye made from the juice of the edible *genipap* fruit to paint their faces. Yanomami men wore black body paint during times of warfare; women who were mourning the loss of a loved one also used black dyes. For red paint they used annato from the pulp of a tropical seed, and for a purple dye they combined anatto with a resin called *carana*. Specific designs and color combinations usually reflected the sex and status of a person, and were always worn during rituals and ceremonies.

Other designs mimicked nature. The Ashaninka of Peru, for instance, writes author-adventurer Joe Kane, "paint their faces with bright orange *achiote*-seed rouge and draw dark cat whiskerlines about the eyes, cheeks, and foreheads."[6] By decorating themselves in this manner, the Ashaninka and other Amerindians hoped to acquire the traits and characteristics of the animal whose appearance they imitated. For instance, a hunter or warrior would paint himself like a jaguar in the belief that this would give him some of the big cat's stealth and power.

Kayapo men were noted for the large wooden disks they inserted through a small

Animals of the Amazon

The Amazon basin is the home of hundreds of animal species, including the jaguar, often called the "king of the jungle," and the largest member of the cat family found outside Africa. Weighing in at two hundred pounds, these large cats are able to climb into the upper levels of the trees but prefer to hunt near streams. Considered sacred, the jaguar is seldom hunted by the indigenous people of the Amazon.

The largest Amazon reptile is the anaconda or boa constrictor, a giant snake measuring up to thirty feet long. It lies submerged in rivers while waiting for its prey and then kills it by squeezing. The indigenous people prize this snake for its food and for its tough skin that is used for making clothing and containers.

Also living in the Amazon are large pigs called peccaries and an animal with hooves called the tapir. The tapir, a relative of the horse and rhinoceros, is remarkable because of its short elephantine trunk that is used to search for food. Both of these animals form an important part of indigenous diets.

The Amazon is also home to the world's largest freshwater fish, the pirarucu (*paiché*) which is over ten feet long and weighs nearly 250 pounds. Better known than this fish, however, is the piranha, a small fish with a deadly reputation. The piranha has jaws filled with triangular, razor-sharp teeth that are designed to slice off bite-sized pieces of flesh. It feeds primarily on other fish but has been known to attack any animal, including man, who enters the water. The fish is capable of stripping a carcass of its meat within a few minutes. Considered a delicacy, the Amerindians of the region have long included this fish as part of their diet.

incision in their lower lip. "The most striking ornamental addition to their attire," one historian writes, "is a light wooden lip disk about two and a half inches in diameter. The disk stretches their lower lip out to produce the Kayapo's extraordinary and very distinctive look."[7] The wearing of such a disk signified the man to be a mighty warrior or hunter.

Many indigenous people of the Amazon practiced body piercing, inserting feathers and bones through their nasal septums. Others scarred their skin by burning self-inflicted wounds with acidic juices to show their ferocity and courage. Permanent tattoos were made by puncturing the skin with palm spines and then applying *genipap* dye. Many Amazonian indigenous people also applied the gum from rubber trees to both their skin and clothing, as the substance virtually waterproofed apparel and offered the wearer protection from the rain.

No less varied than the clothing, cosmetics, and other bodily adornments of the

Amerindians were the ways in which they obtained food for themselves.

Fishing

Fish was the staple diet of those Amerindians who lived along the banks of rivers. The indigenous people employed numerous fishing methods, ranging from the use of spears to more complicated techniques involving the use of poison. Indigenous men did the actual fishing, but the entire family often participated in cleaning and preparing the catch.

The Warao of Venezuela were great fishermen, expert in several different methods, writes historian Josephy, that "ranged from fishing in narrow, rocky gorges with plaited baskets tied to long poles to employing bare hands to pull fish from the mud of shallow pools where they became stranded in the dry season."[8] More efficient, however, especially for large hauls, was a device called a weir. A weir was a fencelike enclosure made of palm fiber which was placed in the current of a stream, trapping hundreds of fish that easily could be speared with multipronged arrows.

The Ashaninka of Peru used the poison of the *barbascu* plant to help them catch fish. They squeezed the poison into a part of the river that had been dammed and then

An Amazonian Indian displays a collection of traditional blowgun darts. The darkened ends show that these have been dipped in poison for hunting.

waited for the stricken fish to rise to the surface where they could easily be captured. The dam was then opened and the river washed away the poison.

Historian Manuel Lucena Salmoral explains how the poison worked: "The poison was obtained from the roots of certain bushes. . . ; baskets containing the poison were placed in back waters, and as the poison became diluted in the water, the fish died and floated up to the surface, where they were easily caught. Once dead, the fish were not poisonous to man."[9]

Using poison to capture fish often resulted in huge catches. As much as a ton of fish might be brought in at one time. In the village it was smoked, salted, sun-dried, preserved, and then shared by the entire community. Most fish were cooked over an open fire; the grilling process helped to neutralize any residual poison.

Hunting

Food was also obtained by hunting, and the jungles of the Amazon provided a ready source of game. Author Mike Tidwell describes the superb hunting skills of the Amerindians: "A vague hoof print on the forest floor, a broken stick in an unnatural position, a line of droppings here, a whiff of odors there—all were part of the expert tracking that led them to their prey as well as led them back out of the jungle."[10] Indigenous hunters used a wide variety of weapons to hunt their prey, including blowguns (a specially designed hollow tube through which poisoned darts were shot), bows and arrows, spears, and traps.

The Yanomami had two hunting methods. The first was called *rami* and provided them with the meat they ate everyday. The other, called *heniyomou*, was a group effort by village men to provide food for special celebrations. Many indigenous societies made a distinction between these two kinds of hunting.

Armadillo, a small mammal covered by armorlike, bony plates, was a favorite target of many hunters, while river turtles and large pigs called peccaries were considered great delicacies. The indigenous people of the forests and jungles also hunted large rodents, monkeys, tapirs, and other animals. Many people, including the Warrau, however, refused to kill large animals such as the jaguar because these animals were considered sacred and thus off-limits to human hunters.

Birds were also a favorite target of indigenous hunters. Most Amerindians, however, took great care not to destroy the bird's feathers. Feathers were such an important part of body adornment, in fact, that hunters used special blunted arrow tips to avoid damaging the bird's plumage.

Food Gathering

In addition to fishing and hunting, the Amerindians were also well known for skillfully utilizing other products of the forest. A wide variety of wild fruits and berries, honey, and various insects were gathered to supplement their diets of fish and meat, for example.

Indigenous gatherers often coiled palm leaves together into a thick rope or used strong vines that were attached to trees as

A Yanomami woman crosses a log bridge with a large basket of fruit on her back. The Amazon rain forest provides a varied diet for indigenous peoples.

The Blowgun

While indigenous hunters used a wide variety of weapons, by far the most common one was the blowgun or blowpipe. The greatest advantage of this weapon was its silence, which gave hunters the advantage of stealth and surprise. A single puff of a blowgun could shoot a dart the size of a large needle into a target more than eight hundred feet away. It was so accurate that warriors could kill a tiny hummingbird in flight.

The Witoto Amerindians, according to historian Manuel Lucena Salmoral in his book *America in 1492*, "made their blowpipes from pieces of palmwood that had been hollowed and fit together. The wood was then polished using a piece of string first soaked in gum and then rolled in sand." The dart, usually made from the back of a palm leaf, was also carefully constructed. The tip of the dart was carved to a fine point and a small notch was made in it so that it would splinter easily on entering the body of an animal.

For most Amerindians, the final addition to the blowgun was curare poison. The tip of the dart was dipped in this poison, made from the sap of the *Strychnos toxifera* plant, and then mixed with ants and poisons from other animals to increase its potency. On entering the bloodstream of an enemy, it caused death by cardiac arrest, paralysis, and respiratory collapse.

climbing aids. Once high in the tree, the gatherer was able to knock clusters of fruit to the ground for easy collection. Many Amerindians were also quite fond of honey. The Kayapo, in fact, cultivated nine different species of bees for the honey they produced.

The Warao of Venezuela gathered white grubs from rotting trees and ate iguanas and their eggs, snails, and turtle eggs. Iguana eggs were collected by poking a stick into the sandy beaches found along the rivers. The men of the village departed as a group in July and August to gather crabs by the thousands among mangrove trees on the rivers. "The men loaded up their canoes," writes Josephy, "and paddled home, blowing conch shells to announce their success. Women boiled the crabs and the feasting began."[11]

Sharing and exchanging were basic to most Amerindian groups with the entire community benefiting from the bountiful food provided by the Amazon. Because of its abundance, the jungle, forests, and rivers were generally hospitable to early settlers. The people quickly found that such communal practices were the best way to survive, and they began to prosper and increase in numbers.

Chapter 2

Amerindian Society and Culture

With their basic needs for food, clothing, and housing satisfied, the indigenous people began to increase in population as they spread across the Amazon basin. Initially living in small, mobile groups, many Amerindians soon settled into communities and allied themselves with neighboring groups to form tribes. Most of these primitive societies were led by a headman, or chief, who relied on the advice of older group members to make decisions. Each Kayapo village, for instance, had at least one chief, chosen for his courage and intelligence, who guided the community. While the early indigenous people of the Amazon did not develop large civilizations like those of the Inca in Peru or the Aztec in Mexico, they nonetheless established social practices and customs that reflected an organized, distinctive society.

Marriage

Marriage became one of the most important ways to form alliances between neighboring groups, for partners generally came from different kin groups or villages. United by common interests, cultures, and languages, these small, neighborhood groups fused into closely-knit communities that ultimately became tribes.

In most indigenous communities, marriages were arranged while children were still quite young by the girl's parents, who selected her future husband and then made an informal but binding contract with the boy's family. At puberty in Warao society, for instance, the boy simply moved in with his bride's parents and lived with them for several years. After the couple produced several children, the young man was given permission to build his own family home.

At this time, the husband was also permitted to take other wives. Many indigenous groups were polygamous and encouraged their male members to have several spouses. These wives were, for the most part, the younger sisters or cousins of the first wife. Wives, the indigenous people believed, got along better if they were blood relatives. The first wife usually held the most important position in the marriage and had the most prestige in the family. Josephy describes this status among the Siriono: "The first wife's hammock was hung to the right of her husband's, the second to the left, the third at his head, and the fourth at his feet."[12] The positions of the hammocks denoted the occupants' position and status in the family.

Roles of Men and Women

The man held the highest status and most power in the indigenous communities and families of the Amazon. Men were typically responsible for all the hunting, fishing, and building, while women tended crops, collected medicinal plants and herbs, cooked, made clothing, and reared children. In addition, men were the spiritual leaders of the community and were also responsible for waging war.

The Tupinamba people of Marajo Island in Brazil actually went out of their way to pamper their men. The head of each household, for example, slept with his wives in a special place in the communal house. During the daytime, the headman sat on carved stools in silence, observing the entire family at work and play. Each adult male was bathed, dressed, painted, and hand-fed. His eldest wife served his meals in special bowls, cups, and plates.

According to the legends of the Mundurucu people of Brazil, however, men were not always the dominant force in indigenous society. In fact, early in their history, Mundurucu women were the leaders of society and held power over everyone else.

Unhappy with this situation, the men devised a way to take control. Josephy writes that they "made a bull-roarer, a piece of flat wood fixed to a string and twirled around the head to make a rushing, humming, or roaring sound. Upon hearing it the women thought it was the sound of a supernatural being and were frightened into submission by the men."[13] Since that time, the Mundurucu community has been male dominated.

Children

In many indigenous societies, men lived separately from their wives. In these communities, young girls lived with their mothers and other female relatives. Between the ages of seven and ten, they were taught to cook, apply body paint, and perform other household chores. Marriage usually occurred when the girl reached the age of ten or twelve.

Indigenous boys, on the other hand, lived with their mothers until around the age of ten, at which time they moved into their father's house. Each boy was assigned to an older warrior or hunter who was responsible for teaching the youth to hunt and fight. Under this apprentice system, boys also learned about tribal rituals and beliefs. When the boys reached the age of fifteen, they "graduated" into the warrior class, where they stayed until they fathered children themselves. The young father then became the head of his own family and was considered an adult.

Becoming an Adult

Most indigenous groups conducted some kind of ceremony or ritual to prepare their

A Yanomami family poses for a photo. Indigenous girls were married by the age of twelve, while boys became adult warriors at the age of fifteen.

male adolescents for adulthood. These rites, according to historians, "clearly sever the bond of childhood and from then on they [the young people] live only in the world of adult responsibility."[14]

Many Amerindian groups used *marake*, the ant test, to accomplish this initiation. *National Geographic* journalist Carole DeVillers describes the ritual used by the Wayana:

Marake begins with dancing and the recounting of myths. The child is given *kasili* [a mild alcoholic beverage] to drink to lighten the ordeal that follows. A *kunana,* a wicker frame with as many as one hundred stinging ants inserted in it, is applied to all parts of his or her body. The recipient is expected to remain silent and still— the ultimate test of a true Wayana.[15]

The ants used in this ceremony are extremely aggressive and their sting is very painful.

A similar kind of initiation was used by the Txukahamei. Writer Carolyn Bennett Patterson describes what she witnessed during her stay with this community: "I learned about the powerful rites that initiate young men into manhood, which include scarifying their legs with fish teeth and holding wasp nests to their hands to demonstrate bravery."[16]

During these various rituals, religious and community leaders chanted prayers to

Birthing Practices

Women in indigenous society usually gave birth unattended or with the help of an older woman in their family or community. While the method of birth and the various rituals that followed the birth differed slightly from society to society, the principles were often similar.

When a Warao woman, for example, began labor, she went to a special hut to await the baby's arrival. Unless the birth was difficult, she delivered her own child. After the child was born, the woman bit through the umbilical cord and tied it off with an ordinary piece of string. The new mother then buried the placenta, or afterbirth, returned to her house, and resumed normal activity, with the added duties of motherhood.

Her husband followed a specific ritual called *couvade* after the birth of his children. For weeks afterward, he spent nearly all of his time in a hammock where he abstained from work, sexual intercourse with any of his wives, and certain foods. By following these rituals, a Warao man ensured, he believed, the well-being of his child.

the spirits, hoping their gods would give the young people courage. Singers and dancers led a celebration following the completion of the ritual.

Festivals and Celebrations

In addition to the rite of initiation, other rituals and ceremonies played an important part of the social life of the indigenous people of the Amazon. These festivities were held for a variety of reasons, including the harvesting of crops and the celebration of community life.

Each year, for instance, the Zaparo of Ecuador celebrated the abundance of the forest. Held between January and March, the festival was, and continues to be, a time for the community to come together to sing, dance, and feast. To prepare for this celebration, a team of the village's best hunters journeyed into the forest while the women prepared feasts of a variety of food and a corn beer called *chicha*.

When the day of the festival came, the women covered themselves with body paint and ornamentation as they waited for the hunters to return. The sound of drums, clay horns, and bone flutes heralded the return of the hunters as they entered the village proudly carrying the game they had killed. Three days of celebration followed.

Puruna Mucushiwa, a Zaparo Amerindian, describes the festivities:

> The first day we danced without stopping and drank great quantities of *chicha*. The second day we ate the meat from the hunt at a great banquet, and we

also danced and drank. The third day . . . when we didn't want to drink anymore, we poured it over our heads, shouting "*imaru, imaru, imaru*, rain, rain, rain." It was a *chicha* rain, a rain of abundance, an offering to the forest.[17]

The Piaroa of Venezuela had a different kind of ritual. Theirs was a rite of forgiveness and cleansing held every year, during which the villagers aired their good and bad deeds for all to hear. Wearing masks and costumes to conceal their identities, community members shared accounts of everything from small kindnesses they had performed or witnessed to such improprieties as infidelity and theft. The villagers listened quietly without condemnation and, at the completion of the ceremony, considered all the deeds honored and cleansed. It was a time of forgiveness and celebration and served to tighten the bonds that held the community together.

Music and Dance

As the various groups of indigenous people formed stable and more permanent villages, they developed a number of traditions and skills that enriched their lives. Many Amerindians, for instance, did ritual dances. Prior to planting, some groups smoked tobacco and vigorously shook various kinds of rattles while dancing and chanting. The purpose of this activity was to expel evil spirits from the fields, and, in the process, improve their harvests.

The indigenous people also used a wide variety of musical instruments. Rattles, pipes,

Large, elaborate costumes adorn these Amazonian dancers during a festival in Brazil. Musicians playing rattles, drums, and a variety of wind instruments usually accompany the dancers.

and drums were common and included a ten-foot pipe called a *urua*, as well as maracas, hollow gourds with a wooden handle that were partially filled with dried seeds or pebbles. Often adorned with parrot feathers, a rattle called a *hebu mataro* was used by the Warao during various religious celebrations.

Two of the most frequently seen and heard instruments among the Amerindians of Venezuela were the *muhusemoi*, a flute made from the bones of a deer, and a handmade violin called a *sekeseke*. The Warao Amerindians played a kind of drum known as the *ehuru*. This hourglass-shaped drum was made from the skin of howler monkeys and was most often used for leading groups of villagers through the forest.

The beat of the drum kept them from getting lost.

The Bororo of Brazil played a kind of clarinet known as the *poari*. This instrument's mouthpiece was made of a narrow cane reed whose upper end was closed and whose lower end was open. The lower end of the reed was then placed inside a large gourd that had been decorated with parrot feathers. Another instrument used by the Bororo was the *culo en tierro*, a drum made from half a coconut husk.

A Creative People

In addition to a rich tradition of music and dance, anthropologists have discovered that the indigenous people found many other outlets for their creativity and skillfulness.

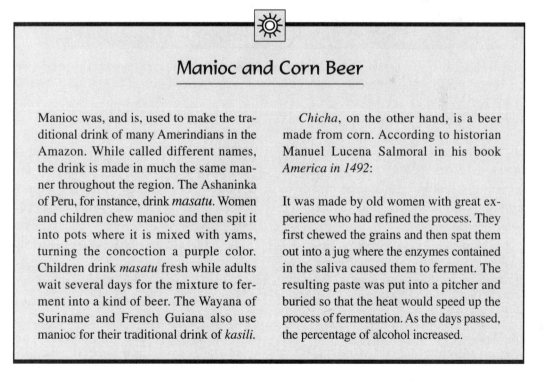

Manioc and Corn Beer

Manioc was, and is, used to make the traditional drink of many Amerindians in the Amazon. While called different names, the drink is made in much the same manner throughout the region. The Ashaninka of Peru, for instance, drink *masatu*. Women and children chew manioc and then spit it into pots where it is mixed with yams, turning the concoction a purple color. Children drink *masatu* fresh while adults wait several days for the mixture to ferment into a kind of beer. The Wayana of Suriname and French Guiana also use manioc for their traditional drink of *kasili*.

Chicha, on the other hand, is a beer made from corn. According to historian Manuel Lucena Salmoral in his book *America in 1492*:

It was made by old women with great experience who had refined the process. They first chewed the grains and then spat them out into a jug where the enzymes contained in the saliva caused them to ferment. The resulting paste was put into a pitcher and buried so that the heat would speed up the process of fermentation. As the days passed, the percentage of alcohol increased.

Archaeologists have unearthed artifacts that challenge the notion that indigenous peoples were backward and primitive. Amazonian Indians continue to produce objects of beauty, such as these headdresses.

Indeed, in the last forty years, various archaeological finds have caused historians to revise earlier theories that depicted the Amerindians of the Amazon as primitive groups with only basic skills and simple societies and cultures.

For instance, archaeologists have discovered large platform mounds on the island of Marajo at the mouth of the Amazon River in Brazil that they believe were once home to over one hundred thousand people. According to scientific testing, the site is over eight thousand years old and was abandoned for unknown reasons sometime in the thirteenth century. The building of platform mounds is often a sign of a more advanced civilization, while the presence of such large populations usually attests to the development of a complex society, far more sophisticated than was previously believed.

Scientists also recovered elaborate ceramic pots that were over eight thousand years old at this same Marajo site, making these items the oldest known pottery in the Americas. Gaspar de Carvajal, a Spanish priest who was a member of the first European expedition to travel the course of the Amazon in the early sixteenth century, described these large jars in his journal: "One hundred gallon storage jars of fabulous quality and artistry rivaling the best in Spain."[18]

Pottery Techniques

The Amerindians of the Amazon, in fact, created a wide variety of pottery and ceramic items. The Assurini of Brazil, who are today considered virtually extinct, have a long history of making an unusual kind of pottery. As of 1999, there were only ten women left in the Amazon who could make this style of pottery. The pottery is characterized by a high gloss made from the natural resin of the *breu do jutai* tree,

while their distinctive red color comes from an extract from the *urucum* plant. What is particularly impressive about this pottery is the extreme thinness of the pots, all of which are handmade without the benefit of any kind of potter's wheel.

The Tukano continue the practice of their ancestors and today turn out very elaborate pottery items. They decorate their ceramics with abstract geometrical patterns that consist of lines, dots, circles, diamonds, and triangles. They also paint various animals and birds on some of their pieces.

The Shuar of Ecuador also make pottery. Even today, they continue to dry their ceramic pieces in the rafters of large smokehouses. After drying for several months, the pots are piled up and covered with firewood.

The seeds of the urucum *fruit, native to the Amazon rain forest, provide the distinctive red coloring of the pottery indigenous peoples created.*

Once the pottery has been hardened, Shuar women decorate the pieces with beautiful designs of faces, flowers, and animals.

Farming

Indigenous skill and ingenuity also extended into other areas of Amerindian life. Many of the indigenous people, for example, became farmers. To clear dense growth for fields, most early farmers used the technique called slash-and-burn, in which several acres of forest are cut down and burned to the ground. The ashes served to fertilize the field for the later planting and harvesting of different crops. Due to the lack of nutrients in the soil in many areas of the Amazon, a field was usually only fertile for two to three years. At that time, the Amerindians usually moved to a new location. The abandoned plots were then allowed to regenerate for many years before they were replanted.

The Yanomami utilized a more advanced farming technique called *conuco* planting. They raised their crops in large, conical mounds called *conucos*, which were packed with leaves to protect the plants from soil erosion. The Yanomami usually planted a variety of different crops to insure that some kind of vegetable would always be growing. The Amerindians worked the soil with sticks, called *coas*, and also used certain fertilizers from

Pest Control and Forest Management

The Amerindians of the Amazon developed many unique and successful ways of managing pests in both their gardens and their homes. Large termite mounds and nests, for instance, are common throughout parts of the Amazon. According to author Mike Tidwell in his book *Amazon Stranger:* "The rock-hard, dried mud, roughly oval-shaped nests would be set afire at dusk and left to burn . . . the faint smoke acting as a . . . repellent to mosquitoes." The Amerindians had learned that the burning mounds release enzymes and other chemicals that keep insects away. Apparently the same chemicals serve the termites themselves by keeping predators away from their nests.

The Kayapo of Brazil discovered a unique way to keep damaging insects off their crops. Several kinds of banana trees, for instance, were often planted around Kayapo crops. The wasps that make their nests in these trees acted as a form of pest management by attacking ants that were capable of eating the crops.

Many scientists consider Kayapo women remarkably adept at forest management. Although the jungle soils are often poor, Kayapo women have, throughout the years, learned to cultivate gardens in different parts of the forest in such a way that it improves the soil at the same time. Certain crops are planted together because some plants have a natural affinity to protect others from insects and weeds.

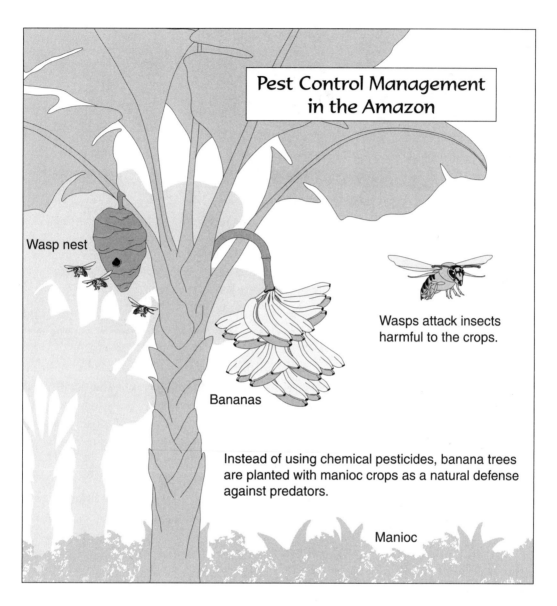

Pest Control Management in the Amazon

Wasp nest

Wasps attack insects harmful to the crops.

Bananas

Instead of using chemical pesticides, banana trees are planted with manioc crops as a natural defense against predators.

Manioc

their cooking fires and the remains of termite nests to enrich the soil.

Crops

The main crop grown by the Amerindians in the Amazon was manioc. Manioc, also called yucca or cassava, is a root crop from which a poisonous juice must be squeezed prior to cooking. Several different techniques were used to make the manioc safe for eating.

The Cofan of Ecuador used a remarkable device called a *fensindeccu* to extract the poison. This implement was made from strips of kapok tree bark that were then

A Blessing Ceremony

The Bororo of Brazil believed that death would occur if they ate new corn or maize before it had been blessed by religious leaders. "The Bororo, [in fact], are firmly persuaded," write historians at the Native American Indian Culture website, "that were any man to touch unconsecrated maize or meat, before the ceremony had been completed, he and his whole tribe would perish."

To ensure that this did not happen, the group's religious leader performed a bless-ing ceremony. The maize was washed and then placed before the holy man who had already prepared himself for the ritual by smoking tobacco or other herbs. After working himself into a kind of trance, he bit into the husk of maize, trembling all over and shouting out from time to time. Once this had been accomplished, the maize was considered safe to eat. A simi-lar kind of ceremony was performed whenever a large animal or fish had been killed.

woven into a hammock-shaped form about three feet long. Handfuls of the crop were placed in the center of this weave while one end was looped over a tree branch.

Journalist Mike Tidwell spent several months with the Cofan. He describes the technique: A Cofan man "took the free end [of the *fensindeccu*], pulled it taut, and began twisting in such a way that the weave enveloped the [manioc] in a squeeze of great force, expelling a stream of cloudy liquid that trickled down to a waiting basin below."[19] The liquid was disposed of while the remaining manioc was made into a mushlike substance and eventually dried and turned into flour used to make pancakes and bread.

Several Amerindian groups including the Tukano used manioc as part of their marriage dowries. Since various clans used different strains of manioc, this tradition fostered wider dispersion and the produc-tion of better crops.

While the basic crop for most Amerindi-ans was manioc, many groups also planted and raised pineapple, papaya, several types of gourds, sweet potatoes, cotton, tobacco, peppers, and a kind of corn called maize. Today, some indigenous people also grow plants that were introduced by Europeans, including bananas, yams, sugarcane, and various kinds of citrus fruits.

Legacy of the Indigenous People

The legacy of the indigenous people of the Amazon is a large and impressive one. The Amerindians invented the hammock, detox-ified manioc, and developed beautiful styles of pottery that are still in use today. In addition, they were also among the first to use the slash-and-burn technique of agriculture, while such staple foods as maize, manioc, potatoes, and squash were all cultivated and harvested prior to European arrival.

Journalist Kathyrn Therese Johnson speaks of these contributions to modern society: "The Indian contributions to . . . [South American] culture [are] most apparent in rural areas and among subsistence farmers, whose style of life is little altered from that of the pre-conquest period."[20]

Today, for example, many rural South American farmers still use a wickerwork tube invented by the Amerindians to squeeze the poisonous sap out of manioc.

Living in extended family communities and tribes, the indigenous people of the Amazon lived, for the most part, happy and productive lives. Their ways of life would continue to flourish for hundreds of years, enriched by a deep spirituality that influenced every aspect of their day-to-day existence.

Chapter 3

Religion, Spirituality, and War

Religion and spirituality were an important part of everyday life in the Amazon. The Amerindians' world was filled with various spirits that guided and influenced everything they did. Even the use of warfare was guided by religious beliefs about the world around them.

A World of Spirits

The natural world of the indigenous people was part of a complex supernatural world of spirits, other beings, and ancestral figures. The Amerindians believed that everything in the natural world was endowed with spirit or soul. These spirits resided in trees, rivers, plants, and animals, and were both respected and feared. These kinds of beliefs form a system of spirituality called animism, that is based on the idea of harmony between humans and the environment.

To avoid offending these spirits, an individual could not take something from nature without leaving a gift or offering of some kind in return. These gifts could be anything from a pinch of tobacco to more elaborate offerings of feathers and personal belongings.

There were also certain unwritten laws or taboos that the indigenous people were careful to observe, for they believed that to ignore a taboo could result in misfortune or illness. For example, Amerindians believed if a hunter killed more animals than his family could eat, the spirits that looked out for the animals would become angry and cause trouble for the hunter and his family.

The indigenous people of the Amazon also believed in ancestral spirits. When the world was young, they believed, many of their ancestors were turned into animals, rocks, or stars. The forests and rivers, as a result, were full of spirits who were once people. Out of respect for these ancestral figures, the Amerindians performed many rituals to solicit the spirits' help in their daily lives.

Shamans

The spiritual leaders of indigenous communities, called shamans, mediated between the people and the spirits in an effort to maintain stability in the Amerindian world. From the earliest days, shamans have been revered as the possessors of an immense knowledge of the supernatural. According to shamanic historian and practitioner Michael Harner, "Shamans . . . are the keepers of a remarkable body of ancient techniques that they use to achieve and maintain well being for themselves and members of their communities."[21]

Throughout the centuries, the shaman has played a central and essential role in Amerindian society. As the keeper of tribal mythic traditions, he has been responsible for guiding the members of his community during such important events as birth, death, and puberty, and for conducting certain initiation rites. Shamans have traditionally functioned as healers as well, entering trancelike states for the purpose of contacting various spirit guides and helpers to assist them in their healing work. Shamans still play a significant role in many indigenous communities of the twenty-first century.

Becoming a Shaman

Becoming a shaman was often a long and difficult process. Most often it was necessary

Mythological Creatures

The indigenous world is full of tales of magical creatures who control various aspects of the surrounding forests and rivers. The early Warao of coastal Venezuela, for instance, lived on a peninsula surrounded by water. They believed that under the world they knew lay another that was inhabited by a double-headed snake whose body encircled the Earth. The snake's movements were believed to cause the ebb and flow of tides.

Historian Manuel Lucena Salmoral, in his book *America in 1492*, explains this kind of belief: "In Amazonia, it was thought that the spirits of the dead wandered in the jungle, taking the form of dwarves, giants, and animals like the *yurupary* (or jaguar) constantly lying in wait to pounce on a man."

Such a figure lives in the forests and is believed to be the cause of all the unexplained noises that come from the jungle. This mythological creature is called the *curupira*, a dwarf whose feet point backward. The Amerindians believe this legendary spirit protects the forest by confusing trespassers with his backward footprints.

The Tupi believe in the *caipora*, a mythological creature who controls the business dealings and fortunes of anyone who looks at it. If a person looks upon this figure, any kind of business or action he or she is performing will turn sour. Some of the indigenous people believe that the *caipora* looks like a small, dark man, while others describe it as a deformed and angry child.

This Amazonian healer uses the herbs of the rain forest to cure disease. Amerindians learned traditional healing arts by apprenticing with a skilled tribal elder.

for the young man, or, in some Amazon communities, the young woman, chosen to assume this important role to serve an apprenticeship with an older shaman to learn sacred songs, tribal secrets, and healing techniques. In addition, the young shaman was taught how to mix and use various hallucinogenic drugs.

Ricardo Pipa, a Tukano Amerindian, was already learning to be a shaman when he went fishing one night. According to Pipa, as he sat on the riverbank he heard a voice calling him from the dark forest. Intrigued, Pipa followed the voice to a tall, pale woman with long blond hair. Later the woman came to the young shaman in his dreams.

Author Sy Montgomery, who interviewed Pipa, describes the novice shaman's experience: "Together they traveled with the dolphins to the great underwater cities of

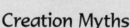

Creation Myths

An important need for human beings throughout the world is to understand how they and their world came into being. The indigenous people of the Amazon have numerous such myths—called creation myths—to explain these concepts.

The Yanomami of Brazil and Venezuela, for instance, believe their ancestors came from the blood of the moon. They tell the story of the moon once living in the body of a shaman. Upon the shaman's death the moon returned to earth and ate the shaman's bones. Angry at this insult, the shaman's relatives attacked the moon with arrows, one of which pierced it, and caused the moon's blood to fall upon the Earth. From the drops of blood, the Yanomami were born.

The Matsigenka of Peru believe they were originally made out of pieces of wood. The powerful creator spirit Makineri cut sturdy trees and brought them to life by singing and breathing on them. And, ac-

cording to author Sy Montgomery in her book *Journey of the Pink Dolphins*, Tukano "legends once told how the first man found a sacred trumpet, and from its music flowed the stars and the wind, the rivers and fish, the forest and game, and all his children."

The Desana of the Colombian Amazon believe that creation occurred when a Creator Sun exploded yellow light into the world. The Sun Father then set about creating the natural world. The Jurana, on the other hand, believe that Sinaa is the mythical father of their community. He is the guardian of a giant stick that holds up the sky. They also believe that when the last Juruna dies, Sinaa will pull down the stick, the sky will fall, and the world will end.

Some indigenous people believe that the Cobra-Grande, or big fish, is a giant serpent who resides in the rivers of the Amazon. This creature supposedly can frighten fishermen away from sacred river locations.

the *Encante* [an enchanted underwater city]. She taught him the *icaros*, the prayers to call the dolphins. . . . The dolphins showed him their prayers."[22] The animals also taught him their medicines and their chants, which Pipa later used in healing ceremonies among his people.

Another shaman, a Shuar *uwishin*, describes this training: "An uwishin's knowledge comes from other uwishins, from dreams, from ceremonies, from passing tests, making many sacrifices, such as tolerating hunger, thirst, heat and cold, sexual deprivation, from years of learning to live alone in the jungle."[23]

The Use of Hallucinogens

The use of hallucinogenic, or mind-altering, drugs has historically been widespread among the Amerindians of the Amazon. Nat-

The Use of Traditional Medicines in Modern Society

Many of the natural medicines discovered by the Amerindians of the Amazon have proven invaluable to modern physicians and researchers. Quinine is perhaps the best-known drug to originate in the Amazon and has been given credit for reducing and even eliminating malaria from many parts of the world.

Curare, the tree resin that is used for poisoning the tips of blowgun darts, is also now in great demand among Western scientists as a medicinal muscle relaxant and anesthetic. Rose periwinkle, a plant that grows only in the Amazon, is now widely used in the treatment of leukemia. "Researchers," writes photojournalist Loren McIntyre in his book *Amazonia*, "believe that the greenheart tree, which has a reputation in the Amazon as an effective contraceptive, [also] has great medical potential."

Most physicians and researchers agree the plant knowledge of the indigenous peo-

ple represents one of the greatest hopes in modern science. They believe that the Amazon and its indigenous people may hold the secrets that will lead to cures for such diseases as cancer and AIDS.

Indigenous knowledge about these natural medicines has saved foreign laboratories and pharmaceutical companies millions of dollars. None of the profits, however, has come to the Amerindians. In May 2000, a group of indigenous spiritual leaders appealed to the Brazilian government to restrict further exploration by foreign scientists. Amerindian leader Marcos Terena spoke for the group and is quoted in the *Kyodo World News Service*: "These companies come to the forest, steal our ancient medicinal knowledge, and amass huge profits manufacturing new drugs." The indigenous people simply want to share in that profit and receive recognition for their contributions to modern medicine.

ural hallucinogens were regarded as sacred and were believed to have magical powers, but their use was not reserved for shamans alone. Every day, Yanomami hunters used a snuff made from *ebene* leaves to sharpen their senses, while the Tukano and Jivaro used a potion made from the *ayahuasca* vine.

Some of these concoctions were smoked, others ingested, some inhaled as snuff, and a few even taken as enemas. The Shuar of Ecuador, for instance, drank a hallucinogenic tea called *natem* and also took *malikawa*, a powerful drug with cleansing properties that the people believed would heal the body.

Another frequently used drug was *nipoco*, a type of snuff extracted from the seeds of a mimosa plant. According to historian Salmoral, "It was placed in the palm of the hand or on a ladle and inhaled through the nose by means of a complicated piece of equipment made of hollow bones, inserted into the nostrils."[24]

But if ordinary people took hallucinogens to enhance their lives, shamans ingested the drugs for more far-reaching purposes. Journalist Elisabet Sahtouris had the opportunity to speak with a Shuar shaman named Marcello, who reported: "When you drink *natem* you see a light clearer than sunlight."[25] During drug-induced trances, a shaman was able to receive helpful advice from spirit guides about healing specific patients.

Curing Illness

Most Amazonian indigenous people believed that breaking a taboo could cause illness. They also feared witches or evil shamans, whom they credited with supernatural abilities to cause the insertion of an object into a victim's body. It was up to the healing shaman to find the cause of the illness and to cure it.

During journalist DeVillers's stay with the Wayana in French Guiana, she had observed a healing ceremony. After villagers rubbed a sick woman's body with a small plant, cotton thread was tied around her elbows, wrists, ankles, and toes. Then the patient was carried to the shaman, who was waiting in a small shelter of palm leaves that had been erected outside the house.

DeVillers describes the remainder of the healing ritual:

> There followed a wild rustling of palm leaves, accompanied by loud sucking and roaring sounds, proof of the violent struggle between the shaman and the *yolok* [evil spirit]. Eventually the shaman emerged carrying what appeared to be a small black pebble, which he said had caused the patient's illness and which he had exorcised from her body.[26]

According to traditional beliefs, shamans can locate such objects in a sufferer's body by supernatural sight, or clairvoyance. During his visit to the Jivaro, Michael Harner was allowed to observe a shaman at work and to note the mind-altering drugs the healer used. He learned that a Jivaro shaman "drinks ayahuasca, green tobacco water, and sometimes the juice of a plant called *piripiri*. . . . The consciousness-changing

This Amazonian Indian shaman strips bark from a tree to use in a herbal healing remedy. Many modern medicines come from plants that only grow in the Amazon basin.

substances permit him to see into the body of the patient as though it were glass."[27]

Traditional Medicine

In addition to the healing performed during trances, shamans in the Amazon also treated illness by using medicines obtained from local plants. The indigenous people of the Amazon, in fact, had a detailed knowledge of the plant world and were able to develop hundreds of herbal remedies for a variety of illnesses. They knew, for instance, which plants to use for snakebite; which to use for cuts, burns, and insect bites; and which to use for fever, vomiting, and pain.

The therapeutic properties of quinine, a drug now used worldwide to treat the high fevers and chills of malaria, were first discovered by the indigenous people of the Amazon. Quinine comes from the bark of the *chinchona* tree. The *retama* plant is still used to make a tea that lessens the effects of yellow fever, while the Ashaninka of Peru use *uncaria tomentosa*, a plant with medicinal qualities that has been proven to boost the immune system.

The *arbol de leche*, or milk tree, secretes a white sap that is believed to increase a man's physical strength and sexual potency. Another useful herbal medicine is the sap from the jaborandi shrub. This drug is used in the treatment of blindness, while a tea made from the leaf of the *juca* shrub eases stomach pains.

Death

While many of these traditional remedies were able to cure some illnesses, other diseases and injuries defied any kind of treatment. Death, therefore, was an ever-present part of indigenous life.

Most of the indigenous people of the Amazon believed in some kind of afterlife. For instance, according to historians the Kayapo of Brazil "believe that at death a person goes to the village of the dead, where old people become younger and children become older."[28] The Warao, on the other hand, believe that an individual's occupation determines a person's after-death destination. Great hunters, for example, were believed to reside in a land rich with game, while skilled craftspeople lived together in happiness while creating magnificent works of art.

The Amerindians also believed that evil spirits, angry over the breaking of taboos, were the primary cause of accidental death. Most other deaths were attributed to somehow failing to appease the spirits.

The indigenous Amazonians believed when a person died, his or her spirit lingered on Earth and could potentially harm its descendants. Burials and funerals, therefore, had to be carried out with the utmost attention paid to rituals and procedures. The Warao, for instance, called on their shaman to perform the acts that were necessary to ensure the dead person's safe passage to the afterlife, while also protecting those left behind. When an elder died, his house was vacated and his corpse was lowered into the river so the fish could pick the bones clean. The skeleton was then placed in the corner of his house along with his personal belongings. Many days or even weeks later, the remains were put into a basket with the skull sitting on top of the rest of the bones. It was not until many months later that the bones were finally buried.

Other Amerindian corpses were wrapped in a hammock, packed in mud, and laid in a canoe called a *wa*. The canoe coffin was then placed above the ground on poles, not far away from the village. Eventually these remains were buried as well.

Other Funeral Rituals

A special kind of burial was performed when a Tucanoa shaman died. He was usually buried in the center of the village *maloca*, where his grave was left untouched for five years. This period of time was believed essential in order for the spot to become sacred and imbued with the shaman's power. "His bones are carefully removed," writes historian Alvin M. Josephy Jr.,

> and the larger one, together with his ornaments and paraphernalia, are placed in a ceramic jar, which is buried in a secret location. The small bones of his fingers, hands, and feet are burned, ground into powder, and mixed with manioc beer, which the men drink to acquire some of his wisdom.[29]

This practice of drinking the corpse's ashes was common to a number of indigenous groups. The Yanomami called this ritual *reahu*. During their ceremony, the indigenous people destroyed the dead person's belongings and then burned his or her bones. At this point, the remains were reduced to ashes and were then added to plantain (a

type of banana) soup. "Symbolically," write Yanomami historians, "this ritual allows the Yanomami to erase all memory of the individual's existence and enable the deceased to disappear completely."[30]

Blood Revenge and Headhunting

Death could also come from injuries sustained in battle. Most of the indigenous societies of the Amazon practiced some form of warfare either as a defensive or offensive tactic. Many groups, in fact, built a way of life based on aggression and war. In nearly all communities, however, war served as an integral part of indigenous spiritual life.

The need for revenge was often the cause of warfare for the Shuar Amerindians of Ecuador and Peru. Wars were fought in response to the death of a relative or community member by an enemy. Relatives of the victim led attacks on the offender with the goal of inflicting "blood revenge." Each death usually initiated a vicious cycle of retaliation in which every death had to be avenged. This resulted in almost constant fighting between communities.

Headhunting, or the practice of killing an enemy and bringing the head back to the community in triumph, had its roots in the concept of blood revenge. The deeds of the Mundurucu of Brazil, for instance, have been recorded in the oral histories of numerous other Amazonian inhabitants. The hunting of human heads became a significant part of this group's religious beliefs. Successful warriors were accorded a sa-

These Yanomami warriors perform a ritual dance for the dead. The ritual ends when the whole tribe eats a soup containing the dead person's ashes.

cred and revered status within the indigenous community and remained honored persons during their lifetimes.

Head Shrinking

Although many Amazonian peoples practiced headhunting, only the Shuar were known for the fear-inspiring practice of head shrinking, called *tsantsa* or *tsantza*. According to Maria Magdelena Kayap, a Shuar Amerindian: "After killing an enemy, the warrior cut off the victim's head and hid himself in the forest, fasting for eight days in order to get ready to prepare the *tsantza* [head]."[31]

While calling on Ayumpum, the Shuar god of life and death, the warrior placed the head in boiling water. The boiling process, in addition to shrinking the head, made it easier for the Shuar to remove the brain and cranial tissue, leaving an empty skull. After the head had shrunk and then dried, the man put hot pebbles inside it to help the facial structures retain their shape, sewed the eyes, ears, nose, and mouth shut, and painted the skin black with charcoal.

With the tips of his fingers he pushed the loose skin around on the skull until the face had resumed its normal shape.

The reason for these preparations, historians write, was "to paralyze the spirit of the enemy attached to the head so that it cannot escape and take revenge. . . . This also prevents the spirit or soul from continuing into the afterlife where it could harm dead ancestors."[32] In addition, by killing an enemy, the warrior symbolically gained possession of the victim's soul and power.

After the Shuar warriors returned home, huge festivities were held to celebrate their victories. These rituals unfolded in three separate phases, each lasting several days, with the last one occurring a full year after the successful battle. The first of these feasts, called "numpenk, involved dancing, singing, and the consumption of large amounts of the fermented corn beer, *chicha*.

During the second feast, the community built each successful warrior a new house. The final and most elaborate feast was

An Amerindian shaman shows two young pupils how to use a shrunken head in rituals. Warriors shrank the heads of their victims to prevent their souls from journeying into the afterlife.

Cannibalism

The Tupinamba, or Tupi, of Marajo Island in Brazil were noted for their ferocity during warfare and their reputation as cannibals. The Tupi considered the eating of human flesh to be a ritual act and an essential part of their spiritual and religious beliefs. "The consumption of human flesh," writes historian Alvin M. Josephy Jr. in his book *America in 1492,* "was an act of supernatural importance and . . . was believed by all to be necessary to ensure the survival of the race and the blessing of the ancestral spirits." Through ceremonial killing and acts of cannibalism, Tupi warriors earned power and prestige.

Prior to warfare, Tupi warriors danced and prepared themselves for battle, donning elaborate feathers and painting themselves. Having abstained from sexual activity in order to establish ritual purity, the warriors set forth at night by land and by canoe. Using fire-burning arrows, they attacked neighboring villages at dawn, capturing and killing as many enemies as possible.

The captives were painted and decorated and then killed with a special club by an appointed executioner. The warriors, including a few, accomplished Tupi women fighters, then drank their victims' blood and ate their flesh. The Tupi also used similar rites when they killed the sacred jaguar. These ceremonies, and others that were preceded by the death of a person or animal, were based on a belief that a warrior could capture an enemy's power as his own.

called the *napin.* At this celebration, the head-takers supplied all the food and drink for the entire community. Abundant food was required, the Shuar believed, or the warrior might lose the prestige he had acquired during battle. Shuar warriors then smeared themselves with blood and danced with the shrunken heads of their enemies. Afterward, the warriors were led to the river where a shaman cut a lock of each man's hair and threw it into the water.

The practice of head shrinking continued well into the twentieth century. In fact, at one time in the 1930s, shrunken heads were so popular outside South America that the Shuar were selling thousands of heads to Westerners for twenty-five dollars each. This led the governments of Ecuador and Peru to pass strict laws that prohibited trafficking of human heads.

Despite the strong spiritual beliefs of the indigenous people of the Amazon and their warlike tendencies, the Amerindians were ill prepared for the events that would occur in the sixteenth century. All their skills, healing techniques, ancestral guardians, and prayers would ultimately fail them as a new and aggressive enemy arrived on the scene.

Chapter 4

Europeans Discover the Amazon

For thousands of years, the various indigenous groups of the Amazon lived in relative isolation. While skirmishes between different tribes of Amerindians occurred with regularity, there was no real outside interference with their ways of life. The Inca of Peru, an advanced civilization located on the western side of the Andes, did make a few excursions into the Amazon, but, for the most part, left the river and forest people alone. As a result, the Amerindians of the Amazon were able to thrive and prosper. Their isolation and the relative peace of the area were shattered in the sixteenth century, however, when a strange ship was sighted near the mouth of the Amazon River.

The Discovery of the Amazon River

Prompted by reports of the famous voyage of Christopher Columbus in 1492, the European maritime powers began exploring the waters and islands of the Caribbean. Gradually, however, their efforts turned southward toward the continent of South America. On one such expedition, in 1499, Spanish navigator Vicente Pinzón located freshwater far out in the Atlantic Ocean. This unusual occurrence led the Spaniard toward the mainland, where he discovered the mouth of a huge river. Unknowingly, Pinzón had found the mouth of what would later be called the Amazon River.

The first Europeans to arrive on the coast of present-day Brazil were not Spanish, however, but Portuguese. They knew of the great river but had no idea where the source of the waterway might be located. A few settlements were made along the coastline, but hostile Amerindians and the forbidding nature of the rain forest discouraged the first settlers from trying to penetrate the interior.

The Search for El Dorado

While Portuguese colonists settled into a new life on the eastern coast of South America and began building sugarcane plantations, the Spanish were busy elsewhere. Under the leadership of explorer Francisco Pizarro, a group of conquistadors invaded the vast Inca Empire of Peru. Caches of gold and other riches, found throughout the Inca lands, were shipped back to Spain. Not long after the conquest of the Inca in the 1530s, a Spanish expedition was formed to cross over the towering mountains in search of more riches. They were searching for the gold of El Dorado.

The Spanish had heard stories of a fabled land and the golden king who lived there since their arrival in South America. Various Amerindian people spoke of a rich kingdom that lay to the east of the mountains. The descriptions of gold and other riches led the Europeans to believe that this land offered even more treasures than those they had found among the Inca. They called this fabled land El Dorado, a term now used to describe any place of fantastic riches.

One of the indigenous groups that claimed knowledge of El Dorado was the Chibcha of Colombia. In the time of their ancestors, Chibcha storytellers told the Spanish, a great meteor fell to Earth and formed a great crater that eventually filled with water. In this lake, called Guatavita today, a group of indigenous people are said to have held initiation rites for their chieftains. According to the legend, the body of the man who was to take the throne was rubbed with a gluelike substance and

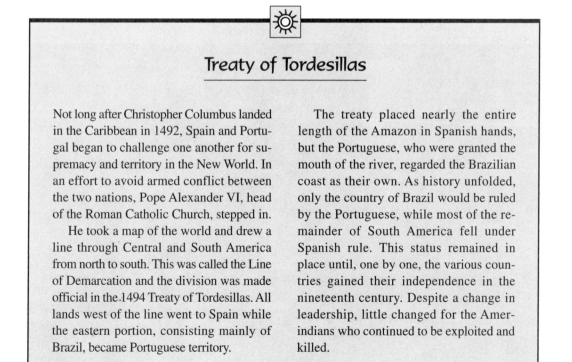

Treaty of Tordesillas

Not long after Christopher Columbus landed in the Caribbean in 1492, Spain and Portugal began to challenge one another for supremacy and territory in the New World. In an effort to avoid armed conflict between the two nations, Pope Alexander VI, head of the Roman Catholic Church, stepped in.

He took a map of the world and drew a line through Central and South America from north to south. This was called the Line of Demarcation and the division was made official in the 1494 Treaty of Tordesillas. All lands west of the line went to Spain while the eastern portion, consisting mainly of Brazil, became Portuguese territory.

The treaty placed nearly the entire length of the Amazon in Spanish hands, but the Portuguese, who were granted the mouth of the river, regarded the Brazilian coast as their own. As history unfolded, only the country of Brazil would be ruled by the Portuguese, while most of the remainder of South America fell under Spanish rule. This status remained in place until, one by one, the various countries gained their independence in the nineteenth century. Despite a change in leadership, little changed for the Amerindians who continued to be exploited and killed.

then covered with gold dust. The gilded leader was then rowed to the middle of the lake along with a raft loaded down with riches and gifts that would be presented to the gods. When the new chief dived off the boat, the water washed away the gold dust that covered his body, after which the gifts and riches were also thrown in the lake. This story and others like it inspired the Spanish to launch numerous missions to find these fabled riches.

A Journey Across the Mountains

Quito, Ecuador, was the place from which the Spanish, under the leadership of Gonzalo Pizarro, the half-brother of the Inca con-queror, mounted their expedition across the mountains. In 1541, Pizarro set out with two hundred Spaniards and over four thousand Amerindians. The trip east over the mountains, however, was far more difficult than the Spanish had anticipated and resulted in the loss of significant numbers of men.

"The expedition," write historians, "struggled over the icy heights of the Andes, then suffered through the continual rain and treacherous slopes of the eastern side of the mountains. Men sickened and died, Indians deserted whenever possible, cattle, pigs, horses, and eventually dogs were slaughtered for food."[33] Facing starvation and death, Pizarro's second in command,

This miniature of El Dorado and his attendants aboard their raft was found in Colombia in 1968. The Spanish explored the Amazon basin in search of El Dorado's riches.

Francisco de Orellana, offered to take a boat and sixty men and go down the river in search of food, little knowing that the waterway would eventually lead him to the Atlantic coast. Orellana hoped to find a friendly group of Amerindians who would offer shelter and emergency rations. Within twenty-four hours, however, it became apparent that the fast-moving river would prevent Orellana from rejoining the main contingent in the near future.

Upon realizing they could not wait for Orellana, whom they feared was dead, Pizarro and his remaining men turned back. After eight days of travel, they happened upon a small village of Amerindians whose people provided temporary shelter and food. In June 1542, sixteen months after leaving Quito, Pizarro and a handful of survivors struggled across the Andes and returned to their home base. Over four thousand men died before the expedition got home.

Meanwhile, unbeknownst to the Spanish, Orellana and his men were still alive and struggling down the mighty river.

Orellana's Voyage

Francisco de Orellana (1511–1546), a close friend and distant relative of the powerful Pizarro family, had journeyed to the Caribbean region in 1527 when he was sixteen years old, eventually ending up in Peru. Orellana was proclaimed a hero for his exploration of the vast South American interior and its many rivers.

Not long after leaving the main expedition, Orellana and his men did indeed find a friendly group of Amerindians. They stayed with this indigenous group for several weeks, eating, resting, and regaining their strength. Talking to his hosts, Orellana discovered that he was in the midst of territory recognized by the indigenous people as inhabited by a confederation of tribes called Aparia.

The Aparia, Orellana found, engaged in long-distance trade and, as a result, were able to give the explorer very useful information about what lay ahead on the river. After two months, during which they repaired their boat and built another one, the Spanish expedition set out again. The Apari women also provided Orellana's group with a wide range of local food, including turtle, fish, and forest animals.

This initial contact with the Amerindians was, for the most part, a friendly and nonviolent one. Orellana's men remarked on the intelligence and ability of the Amerindians. The Europeans assumed, however, it was their right to dominate the native people and to take any land or other possessions they liked. Thus, they claimed the Apari village and the surrounding area on behalf of the Spanish monarch and gave the indigenous people a lecture on Christianity.

Reactions of the Indigenous People

The indigenous people Orellana and his men encountered during the trip reacted variously. Some fled in terror, while others provided food and shelter. Many others attacked with clubs and spears. For the indigenous people of the Amazon, these first

Other Explorations of the Amazon

The first expedition to begin at the mouth of the Amazon on the Atlantic coast of South America and travel all the way to its source, high in the Andes, was led by Portuguese general Pedro Teixeira in 1637 and 1638. Unable to establish settlements along the way because of overwhelmingly hostile Amerindians, Teixeira nonetheless completed the journey and returned to the Atlantic coast with a contingent of over a thousand men.

His mission was intended, in part, to combat the increasing pressure of the British and Dutch who had begun building forts along the lower Amazon. Claiming the interior for the Portuguese, the explorer reported to his superiors that the Amazon was rich in gold and silver. While his statement was sheer exaggeration, his enthusiasm helped fuel the already–intense rivalry between Spain and Portugal.

No further explorations were carried out along the Amazon until the nineteenth century, when scientists began exploring the natural beauty and abundance of the region. Englishman Henry Walter Bates spent eleven years in the interior of the Amazon between 1848 and 1859, and amassed the single largest collection of insects ever made in the region by an individual scientist.

Since then, the river and forests have been explored by countless others, including an expedition led by former American president Theodore Roosevelt in 1914, and others sponsored by such organizations as the National Geographic Society and the Smithsonian Institution.

contacts with the Europeans became increasingly tragic and violent.

Hundreds of indigenous people were killed for challenging the Spaniards' right of passage down the river, while others were hanged to show the Amerindians that the Spanish would not tolerate any acts of disobedience or disrespect. In many cases, the explorers provoked fights by stealing food and canoes from the Amerindians, a pattern that was to become common in South America and elsewhere.

As the explorers moved farther down the big river, they encountered more heavily-settled areas and larger communities of Amerindians. The Omagua, for example, were one of the most accomplished people the voyagers met. This group impressed Orellana with their roads, storage tanks filled with turtles, ample food supplies, and the large, ceramic jars they crafted. Nevertheless, friendly relations did not last long and the explorers soon wore out their welcome by stealing food and other supplies from the Amerindians. The Omagua are now largely gone, wiped out by Western disease, warfare, and European persecution.

The Women Warriors of the Amazon

In the Imara village, farther downriver, Orellana and his men began to hear rumors about the existence of a fierce tribe of female warriors. A skirmish with these women allegedly occurred on June 24, 1542, and was reported by Gaspar de Carvajal, the priest who accompanied Orellana and kept journals about the journey. He describes the warriors in his diary: "We ourselves saw these women who were there fighting . . . with their bows and arrows in their hands, doing as much fighting as ten Indian men."[34]

The Spaniards named these women after a similar group of women warriors from Greek mythology called the Amazons, a name that Orellana would give to the region and the great river. The editors of Time-Life Books pin down the connection: "Such a foe, the Spaniards were quick to conclude, could only be the Amazons, the mythical tribe of women that Columbus and other explorers believed ruled the dark jungles of the New World."[35]

For hundreds of years, historians have questioned the existence of the women warriors. Within the last forty years, however, archaeologists have found evidence that supports the legends of female fighters in the Amazon. Many of the Amerindians of the region also recount stories of their existence and still hold ceremonies and dances to celebrate the mysterious women warriors of old.

Completion of the Journey

After completing the four-thousand-mile trip down the Amazon, Orellana and his men reached the mouth of the river and the Atlantic Ocean on August 26, 1542. Their next task was reaching the nearest Spanish settlement, an area that lay over twelve hundred miles to the northwest in the Caribbean. After rebuilding their ships, the Spaniards

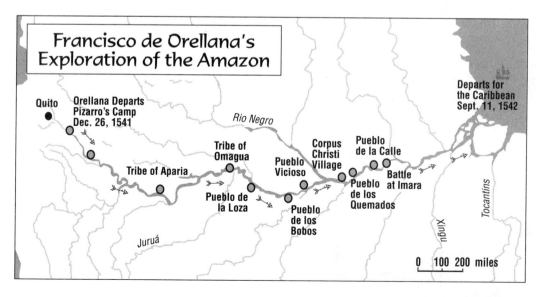

Francisco de Orellana's Exploration of the Amazon

Quito

Orellana Departs Pizarro's Camp Dec. 26, 1541

Rio Negro

Departs for the Caribbean Sept. 11, 1542

Tribe of Omagua

Tribe of Aparia

Pueblo de la Loza

Pueblo Vicioso

Corpus Christi Village

Pueblo de la Calle

Battle at Imara

Pueblo de los Quemados

Pueblo de los Bobos

Juruá

Xingu

Tocantins

0   100   200 miles

left the river, entered the Atlantic, and, on September 11, reached Spanish land.

Upon his return to Spain shortly thereafter, Orellana met with the monarchs and other court officials. With gross exaggerations of his voyage and the riches he had discovered, the explorer obtained a commission to conquer the regions of the Amazon. He was told by the Spanish monarchs to return to the river and establish a colonial presence for Spain in the region. Orellana arrived off the Brazilian coast before Christmas in 1545 with four hundred men and a grant naming him governor of the Amazon.

Disaster quickly struck the expedition. Approaching the area from a different direction—the Atlantic—Orellana could not find his river. He soon became lost and died along with his men at an unknown spot

This woodcut depicts the cruel treatment of the South American Indians under Spanish colonialism. Forced to work on Spanish plantations, the Indians were reduced to slavery.

The Encomienda System

All the land in Ecuador, Peru, and other Spanish colonies was distributed by the Spanish monarchs under the *encomienda* system. Starting with King Ferdinand and Queen Isabella, the rulers of Spain granted certain subjects the rights to occupy and use large tracts of land, along with the labor of the Amerindians who happened to be there. The majority of early grantees were members of the Spanish nobility who acquired the land for the purpose of building plantations and cattle ranches. While part of the profits from these ventures returned to the monarchy, most of the income remained with the landowners. In return for the land grants, the Spanish colonists were charged with protecting the indigenous people and converting them to Christianity.

The Roman Catholic Jesuit priests were also given land to develop. While they did instruct the Amerindians in Christianity, the harshness of their methods often increased in proportion to the people's resistance to their teaching. The other settlers, however, did the exact opposite of protecting, turning the indigenous people into slaves who were required to give the landowners a large share of their crops and hunted animals. Even young children, pregnant women, and elders were forced into working in intolerable conditions. Thousands of Amerindians died.

sometime in late 1546. Because of the reports given by Orellana and others that the indigenous people were well established and well armed, the Spanish decided to forgo any further exploration or settlement of the Amazon at that time. In any event, Spain's rival, Portugal, had gained a foothold on the Atlantic coast of Brazil even before Francisco Pizarro's conquest of the Inca.

Enslavement of the Amerindians

After the arrival of Portuguese explorer Pedro Alvars Cabral in what would later become the country of Brazil in 1500, the Portuguese had established several large settlements along the Atlantic coast. Within a few years, they turned to large-scale plantation farming and the cultivation of sugarcane. As this industry grew, a larger labor force was needed. The Portuguese turned to those Amerindians who lived in the nearby jungle.

The Portuguese began to send out slave hunters called *bandeirantes* into the Amazon. These unscrupulous men ranged far into the rain forest in search of Amerindians who could be used in the cane fields of northeast Brazil. Thousands of indigenous people were captured and forced to work the land, toiling in the hot tropical sun under extremely adverse conditions. Most died from illness, overwork, and starvation. Many indigenous communities fought the *bandeirantes* while others fled deeper into the jungle.

The Portuguese also realized the value of many of the trees in the rain forest. Of particular value was mahogany, an extremely hard wood that does not rot, and brazilwood, a wood that is used to make a red dye. Thousands of other Amerindians were enslaved to cut down these trees and transport them to the coast for shipment to Europe. The captured indigenous people were held in crowded, unsanitary camps in the jungle where they were ill-treated and poorly fed. Hundreds more died.

As the number of Amerindians available for slave labor dwindled, the Europeans began to turn toward Africa. In the ensuing years, hundreds of thousands of Africans were shipped to South America where they were forced to work in the cane fields and in the rain forests. In 1888, Brazil outlawed the practice of slavery, which, by then, was illegal almost everywhere in the world.

Missionary Activity

In these early years, many missionaries tried to help the indigenous people fight off the *bandeirantes'* attempt to enslave them. In Brazil, for instance, Roman Catholic Jesuit missionaries built missions and began supplying arms to the indigenous people. The Jesuits and the Amerindians, however, never completely succeeded in stopping the slavers' raids.

The Jesuits focused primary efforts, however, on converting the indigenous people to Christianity and educating them. They eventually created a system of Amerindian villages called *aldeias* to help facilitate this process. By the late sixteenth century, the Jesuits had gathered together thousands of Amerindians and were teaching them the fundamentals of Christianity. The priests also attempted to impose European agricultural techniques on people whose traditional methods of farming had been very successful. The new ways never took hold, though, and, in 1759, a conflict of viewpoints about the indigenous people came to a head and the Jesuits were expelled from Brazil by the Portuguese government.

Other missionaries also encouraged the indigenous people to change their beliefs, often using force and violence in their attempts to gain converts. Hundreds of Amerindians were whipped and beaten to keep them from practicing their traditional beliefs, while, in addition, food and other supplies were withheld to coerce attendance at church. These practices caused the Amerindians to feel cheated and discriminated against. Nor did the indigenous people understand many of the concepts and customs that were introduced by the missionaries. Many Amerindian communities reacted with hostility to the continued disapproval of their customs.

As a result, only a few missionaries were able to successfully settle among the indigenous people. For the most part, the Amerindians remained isolated in remote jungle areas where they continued to observe their traditional ceremonies and other spiritual practices.

A painting shows a group of Amerindians interacting with European colonists. Early colonists to the Amazon typically wanted to change the traditional lifestyles of the Amerindians.

The Amerindians Fight Back

Several groups of Amerindians were successful in keeping outsiders from their territory during these early years of exploration and colonization. The Cofan of Ecuador, for instance, were very effective guerrilla fighters who eventually caused the Spanish to retreat from Cofan territory.

The Ashaninka of Peru first appear in the historical record in 1635, when Franciscan missionaries from Spain pushed into the Amazon in search of people to convert to Christianity. Initially friendly, the Ashaninka were quickly decimated by disease. The survivors, unwilling to suffer any longer under the often-abusive treatment of the Europeans, rose up against the intruders, burning missions and killing priests. According to writer Joe Kane, "Under . . . Juan Santos de Atahuallpa, they drove missionaries completely out of . . . Peru and the difficult terrain and their fierce reputation kept their territory free of outsiders for . . . years."[36]

Early Spanish explorers also encountered the fierce Shuar of Ecuador and Peru, who, in 1599, banded together, killing thousands of Europeans in a period of several months. This onslaught and the Shuar practice of head shrinking discouraged outsiders from entering their territory for many years afterward.

Results of Early Colonization and Exploration

When the Europeans came to the Amazon, most of them wanted to conquer, use, or change the forest and the Amerindians in

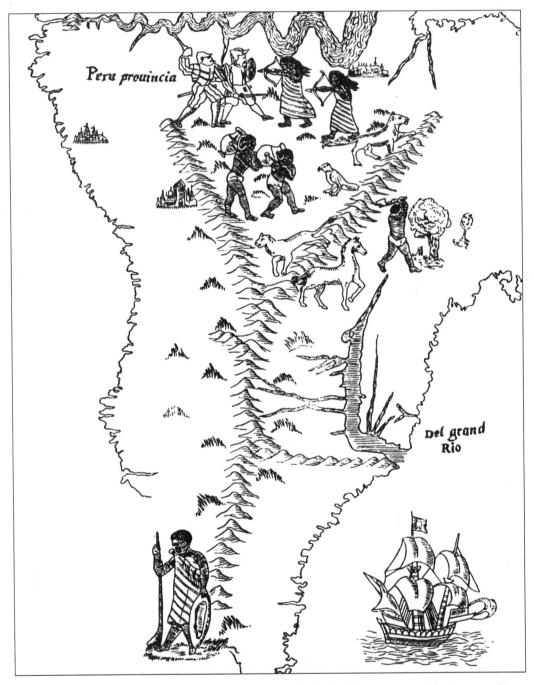

This sixteenth-century map of South America shows the Andes Mountains and the Amazon River. The map also depicts the armed conflict between the Spanish and the natives.

some way. They accomplished these goals with brutal efficiency. When the indigenous people did not bend to the colonists' will, they were killed summarily, by neglect, or by such stealth methods as giving them poisoned food and clothes that had been infected with communicable diseases. "In the jungles of Brazil," writes journalist Tim Cahill, "there had been genocidal tragedies: Amazonian Indians given blankets infected with measles, sugar laced with arsenic."[37]

Hundreds of thousands of Amerindians died of European diseases against which they possessed no immunity. Measles, tuberculosis, smallpox, and even the common cold wiped out entire villages. These diseases decimated the Amerindian population of the Amazon. Out of an estimated population in the millions at the beginning of the sixteenth century, only 10 percent of that number survived the first fifty years of European occupation and exploration. With this great decrease in population, social structures and leadership hierarchies that had served for thousands of years were destroyed or disrupted.

While isolated excursions by explorers and missionaries into the Amazon rain forests continued during the seventeenth and eighteenth centuries, the area remained largely unmapped and unexplored. The ferocity of the indigenous communities and the inaccessibility of most of the Amazon forestalled any widespread efforts to settle or conquer the region.

Suffering widespread loss of life as a result of disease and enslavement, many Amerindians fled deeper into the jungle, where they remained for the next two hundred years. The Europeans were, for the most part, content to concentrate their efforts on colonizing the coastline of South America and the territory to the west of the Amazon. The indigenous people of the area, meanwhile, continued their traditional practices and hoped they had seen the last of the invaders. Their situation was to change for the worse, once again, toward the latter half of the nineteenth century.

Chapter 5

Opening Up the Amazon

For several hundred years after the initial settlements were made in South America, the government of Brazil, which controlled most of the vast Amazon basin, was reluctant to open up that area to shipping and exploration by other countries. "The Portuguese monarch and its Brazilian successors," writes historian Marshall C. Eakin, "have long feared that the other European powers or the United States would try to wrest Amazonia and its riches from them. In the mid–nineteenth century, only after great pressure from the United States and Great Britain did the Brazilian monarch open up the river to international shipping."[38]

Perhaps as many as a million Amerindians had survived into the twentieth century, largely due to their isolated locations. The opening of the Amazon changed their situation forever.

The Rubber Boom

The primary impetus for the opening of the Amazon increased world demand for the rubber that was needed for use in the ex-

panding tire and automobile industry. As had happened hundreds of years earlier, outsiders in large numbers began to descend on the interior of the Amazon and turned to the indigenous people for labor.

During the rubber boom that occurred at the beginning of the twentieth century, hundreds of thousands of Amerindians were captured and put to work tapping rubber trees. The Ashaninka of Peru were one of those communities most severely affected. They suffered terrible loss of life and, in the process, also lost their land and their freedom. "In Peru, to punish workers who fell short of their quota," writes author Sy Montgomery of one atrocity, "one [Peruvian] overseer [working for an American company] ordered a massacre of Indian children and then cut them up for food for the guard dogs."[39]

The rubber boom in the Amazon came to an abrupt end in the 1920s. Many years earlier, seeds from Amazon rubber trees had been sent to Malaysia in the Far East for planting. The seeds thrived in the

Amazon Indians bring food to market by canoe. The opening of the Amazon basin to outside trade in the mid–nineteenth century spelled doom for indigenous cultures.

Modern Rubber Tapping

Despite the lower price of Far Eastern rubber, there are still over one hundred thousand rubber tappers working in the Amazon today. Most of these are independent peasants and Amerindians who hope to sell their products to international companies.

The Portuguese word for rubber tapper is *seringeiro*. The men who do this work collect latex, a white liquid that later hardens into an elastic, dark, gluey material. This harvesting is done in the same manner that farmers tap a maple tree for sap. A small cut is made in the bark of a tree and a cup is attached to catch the dripping latex. Rubber tappers visit dozens of trees a day, returning later in the day or evening to collect the latex. Many work in the evening or night, wearing a headlamp, to take advantage of the increased latex flow that happens in the dark.

Because of the recent threat of deforestation, the tappers and the Amerindians of South America have joined forces to defend the rain forest. This effort against further exploitation resulted in the formation of the Forest People's Alliance, an organization dedicated to preserving the rain forest.

nutrient-rich soil there, resulting in the production of tremendous amounts of rubber. It quickly became too expensive to extract the rubber in the jungles of the Amazon, where growing conditions had always been far from ideal.

Twentieth-Century Changes

After the end of the rubber boom in the 1920s, the Amazon and its inhabitants again remained largely undisturbed for another fifty years, except for a few, sporadic incursions by outsiders. According to photojournalist Loren McIntyre: "The forests of Amazonia still stood 99% intact four centuries after the Europeans arrived, since almost all travel and settlement was river-ine. But when overland trails widened into vehicular roads during the twentieth century . . . trees began to fall."[40]

With improved transportation networks, the Amazon was soon opened to all comers, not only individual settlers but small and large companies determined to dig for gold, drill for oil, and establish vast cattle ranches. These North Americans and Europeans almost immediately began to encroach on not only the Amazon's natural forest reserves but on the region's indigenous people as well. Author Tim Cahill explains: "The [indigenous] people are driven from the forest by mining operations, by giant ill-conceived cattle ranching schemes, by enormous agricultural projects. They [now] stand alongside the road where the forest once stood."[41]

Road Building

The construction of roads in the Amazon has been a very controversial issue. Not only has it led to the destruction of hundreds of thousands of acres of rain forest, but road building has also resulted in the loss of animal habitats and the displacement of hundreds of indigenous communities.

The eleven-thousand-mile-long Trans-Amazon Highway, the first project undertaken, was constructed across the jungles and rain forests of the Amazon in the 1960s at the expense of millions of acres of forest and the forced resettlement of dozens of in-digenous groups. The building of this road took over twenty years to complete but has, in the last ten years, been largely abandoned. Proving too lengthy and too expensive to maintain, it now lies in ruins in many parts of the Amazon.

One of the largest incursions into the Amazon was the Carajas Project, a multi-billion-dollar development scheme announced by the Brazilian government in the late 1950s. This project included the building of roads; the development of mines for iron ore, gold, and copper; the construction of a huge chemical fertilizer plant; the opening of ten new cities; two immense colonization projects, officially intended to provide land for poverty-stricken residents

This 1972 photo shows a portion of the Trans-Amazon Highway, with felled trees flanking it on either side.

of crowded cities; and the building of numerous dams. This project, aimed at utilizing the resources of the Amazon, was primarily undertaken to provide much-needed money for the Brazilian government to pay off massive foreign debts.

Dam Building

During the late 1950s, 1960s, and 1970s, numerous dams were built along the Amazon and its tributaries. These hydroelectric projects were undertaken by various South American countries to provide electricity for towns throughout the region, as well as to divert water for use in industries along the rivers.

The benefits these projects produced were small when compared with the devastation the dams caused to the Amazon and its inhabitants. The dams flooded thousands of square miles of forest and displaced previously undisturbed Amerindian communities. As the indigenous communities moved out, other groups moved in. Prospectors in search of gold and drilling companies looking for oil poured into the once-isolated Amerindian territory.

By the 1990s, the Brazilian government was receiving worldwide criticism for the destruction these projects were causing. In 1996, Brazil announced plans for less damaging development and dropped its plans to build eighty new dams.

Colonization

Encouraged by the publicity accompanying the Carajas Project, tens of thousands of landless peasants from Brazil, dreaming of

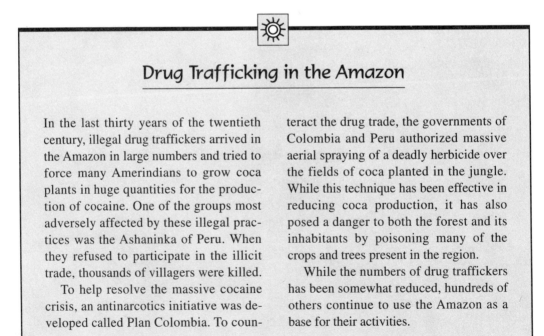

Drug Trafficking in the Amazon

In the last thirty years of the twentieth century, illegal drug traffickers arrived in the Amazon in large numbers and tried to force many Amerindians to grow coca plants in huge quantities for the production of cocaine. One of the groups most adversely affected by these illegal practices was the Ashaninka of Peru. When they refused to participate in the illicit trade, thousands of villagers were killed.

To help resolve the massive cocaine crisis, an antinarcotics initiative was developed called Plan Colombia. To counteract the drug trade, the governments of Colombia and Peru authorized massive aerial spraying of a deadly herbicide over the fields of coca planted in the jungle. While this technique has been effective in reducing coca production, it has also posed a danger to both the forest and its inhabitants by poisoning many of the crops and trees present in the region.

While the numbers of drug traffickers has been somewhat reduced, hundreds of others continue to use the Amazon as a base for their activities.

Dead trees along the Amazon testify to the destruction of the rain forest caused by development, in this case by flooding from a dam built for a hydroelectric plant.

buying their own small farm, also began streaming into the opened areas. The vast majority of land, however, went to large landowners. Fences sprang up around huge cattle ranches and trees were felled and burned at an astounding rate, resulting in further devastation to the rain forest. To make matters worse, thousands of low-income settlers who had managed to obtain some acreage were frustrated by the nutrient-poor soil of the region, which forced them to clear larger and larger swaths of forest to find tillable land. Scientists have estimated that by 1990 deforestation had already destroyed nearly 15 percent of the Brazilian rain forest.

The majority of these poor farmers were *caboclos*, people of mixed Portuguese and Amerindian heritage. Today they live in simple, palm-thatched huts in much the same manner as the traditional indigenous people. Many of their homes have no electricity, no running water, and no sewage disposal. The *caboclos* plant manioc and other crops and have little access to schools or medical care. Many survive by becoming rubber tappers or by using simple fishing and hunting techniques. The Brazilian government has done little to help them. While some low-rent housing has been provided, the *caboclos* continue to face nearly insurmountable problems.

As the twenty-first century opened, the number of settlers in many areas far exceeded the number of indigenous people. The slow but steady entry of outsiders into the interior of the Amazon has put tremendous pressure on the Amerindians. "By one estimate," writes Eakin, "contact with whites decultured or destroyed more than eighty tribes between 1900 and 1957."[42]

Creation of Reserves and Reservations

To make room for the thousands of colonists moving into the Amazon, hundreds of different indigenous groups were resettled on various reserves and reservations. On paper the total acreage set aside for reservations is substantial. As of 1997, for instance, Amerindian reservations officially covered nearly 10 percent of Brazil's total land area.

Despite promises of governmental support and protection, however, a large portion of Amerindian reservation land has been taken over by South American governments during the last forty years. "Merely establishing a reserve," writes Montgomery, "does not guarantee its protection; regulations do not ensure that the government enacting them will either enforce or even obey its own laws. Much of the land is protected on paper only."[43] There is, in fact, virtually no government presence on most of the reservations.

In addition, many of the reserves are not protected by any kind of police force. This makes it easy for miners, loggers, and oil companies to trespass on indigenous land. The Brazilian government, for instance, conducts periodic sweeps to root out gold prospectors on Yanomami land. While they have had some success, the operations have limited funding, and when the money runs out the miners come back. In addition, the governments of South America often

A Brazilian tribal chief uses a satellite telephone to place a call from his reservation. In recent years, South American governments have reclaimed land originally set aside for such reservations.

ignore treaties and use indigenous land for road building and other projects.

Anti-Indigenous Attitudes

Many oil companies, mining and lumber companies, and government organizations, along with the majority of nonindigenous South Americans, believe that the Amerindians of the Amazon are actually preventing progress. They question why so much land is being set aside for such a small percentage of the population. Amerindians in Brazil, for example, represent less than 0.2 percent of the total population of that country, while "controlling" 10 percent of the land.

Many politicians, policemen, army officers, ranchers, and colonists actively resent the Amerindians. Writes journalist Michael S. Serrill:

The non-Indian majority of people in the Amazon region condemn the government [of Brazil and other countries] for protecting the Indians too well by handing them huge swaths of land . . . and blocking outsiders from exploiting gold, diamonds, tin, and other riches. The miners may be an unruly bunch, but they bring jobs and taxes, while the Indians are regarded as backward and ignorant.[44]

Oil company workers attempt to clean up an oil spill in an Ecuadorian river. Oil drilling in the region is on the rise despite native resistance.

The prevailing opinion, in fact, contends that the indigenous people are inferior in every way to the remainder of the population. From the days of Columbus, most Westerners believed that the New World was populated by uncivilized and primitive people. Displaying the cultural arrogance of the time, the Europeans labeled as savages the non-Christian indigenous people whose ways were so unlike their own.

In the late twentieth century, nonindigenous South Americans, Europeans, and others would rely on these arguments and viewpoints to defend the taking of indigenous land and many of the other policies undertaken in the Amazon. Even as recently as the 1980s, when *National Geographic* journalist Carole DeVillers planned a trip to the Amazon, she was greeted with these remarks: "You're going alone? You're out of your mind! First thing you know, you'll be raped. You'll have to pay for every picture you take of the Indians. They'll shoot arrows at you, they'll steal your belongings."[45]

The Discovery of Oil

Incursions into indigenous lands intensified when major oil reserves were discovered in the Ecuadorian rain forest in the late 1960s. Helicopters, transport planes, flotillas of boats, and thousands of workers from the Texaco–Gulf Oil Company descended on the Cofan homeland and immediately began testing for oil. Drilling continued off and on for the next thirty years with varying degrees of success. Another major oil discovery in the early 1990s intensified "outside" interest in Cofan lands.

The early 1990s, for instance, had seen the establishment of the Cuyabeno Wildlife Reserve in Ecuador. This park was developed for the use of the indigenous Amerindians and, on paper at least, was off-limits to South American developers and international industries. Less than two months after the reserve was made official, a seismic oil testing crew from a U.S. company was in the area.

This new oil discovery led the Ecuadorian government to open the park for exploration and drilling on lands previously held specifically for indigenous use. The country was under pressure to pay off massive foreign debts, and, within a few years, the reserve had been inundated by oil drillers. Despite numerous protests from the Cofan and other Amerindians, and without seeking permission from the indigenous communities, the oil companies simply moved into the rain forest. Over the past decade, oil production and oil field development have continued to increase in Ecuador.

The Cofan Fight Back

The Cofan, one of the oldest surviving indigenous cultures of the Amazon, make their home in the northeastern part of Ecuador. In the last thirty years, this group of Amerindians has become well known for their efforts to rid their homelands of oil drillers.

Randall B. Borman, the son of American missionaries, grew up among indigenous people and was later elected chief of the Cofan village of Zabalo. Borman has been at the forefront of Cofan efforts to fight the oil companies. Borman describes the goal of the Cofan: "What we are working

Randy Borman

Randall B. Borman was born in 1955 in the rain forest of eastern Ecuador to missionary parents who were working with the Cofan Amerindians. He grew up playing with indigenous children and speaking their language fluently. Borman and his Cofan wife, Amelia, live today with their two children in the village of Zabalo.

Borman left Ecuador briefly in 1973 to attend college in the United States but soon dropped out so he could return to the Amazon. At that time, he found the indigenous community struggling against big oil interests. He began to work with the Cofan to defend their territory and was ultimately appointed their chief.

Writer Mike Tidwell visited Borman and describes his appearance in his book *Amazon Stranger*. Borman is, he writes, "an American . . . born and raised among forest Indians, a blowgun hunter since age four, a man gone totally native. With paint on his face and wild boar eyeteeth strung around his neck, [he] was leading the [Cofan] Indian campaign to keep the oil intruders out."

Borman has also encouraged the Cofan to become self-sufficient by forming an ecotourism company and engaging in scientific and other kinds of research. He continues to guide the Cofan in their struggle against the oil companies.

for here in Zabalo is the survival of a people, survival of a culture, and the survival of an environment."[46]

The most crucial test for the Cofan came in 1993, when an operating well was found deep within the forest. Borman led the indigenous community to the isolated well with shotguns and spears, surrounded the site, and told the foreman to stop drilling. The foreman complied but also notified the Ecuadorian military, who responded with soldiers wearing battle fatigues and carrying automatic weapons. After a brief standoff, the military and the national oil company, Petroecuador, backed down and cleared out.

Despite this effort and many others, oil drilling continues on Cofan homeland. As the twenty-first century opens, these Amerindians are continuing their fight against overwhelming odds and attempting to work with the government of Ecuador to control environmental damage to their land.

Gold Mining

The next incursion into indigenous land occurred in the late 1980s, when huge deposits of gold were found in the interior of the Amazon. Thousands of miners swept into the homeland of the Yanomami Amerindians, bringing with them violence and epidemics of various diseases. Despite the fact that the Yanomami were living on a "protected" reserve, the Brazilian government ultimately yielded to the pressures of the miners and, by the late 1980s, had given permission for what turned out to be no less than an invasion of Yanomami territory.

Conflict between the Amerindians and miners began almost immediately and gradually intensified. The world's attention was drawn to the region in 1993, when reports of an atrocity surfaced. One among many journalists who exposed the event was Michael S. Serrill, who writes: "An unknown number of forest-dwelling Yanomami Indians are missing and presumed murdered, victims of rampaging gold miners."[47]

News of the massacre came from indigenous survivors who sought refuge at government outposts. They reported that gold miners had invaded their village, slashing the throats of women and children and mutilating their bodies. A team of Brazilian investigators later discovered more than seventy mutilated Amerindian bodies, drawing these remarks from UN secretary-general Boutros Boutros-Ghali: "This tragic event, which took place during the International Year of the World's Indigenous Peoples, puts in relief the plight of indigenous people around the world."[48]

Yanomami chief Davi Kopenawa later spoke on behalf of his people:

I am appealing for help for the Yanomami people—we are asking people to send letters to the Brazilian government urgently asking for the removal of all gold miners from our lands.

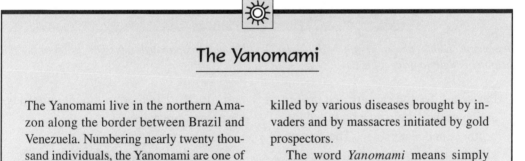

The Yanomami

The Yanomami live in the northern Amazon along the border between Brazil and Venezuela. Numbering nearly twenty thousand individuals, the Yanomami are one of the largest remaining indigenous groups in South America. They also have the distinction of being one of the few tribes that still retain, for the most part, a traditional way of life.

Up until the 1980s, the Yanomami had had very little contact with the outside world. Since 1987, however, about 10 percent of their population has been killed by various diseases brought by invaders and by massacres initiated by gold prospectors.

The word *Yanomami* means simply "human being." When first contacted by outsiders, they greeted visitors with drawn bows. Anthropologist Napoleon Chagnon was among the first to visit one of their villages. In a *National Geographic* article entitled "Yanomamo, the True People," he wrote: "I looked up and gasped when I saw a dozen burly naked men staring at us down the shaft of their drawn arrows."

Yanomami shaman and environmental activist Davi Kopenawa appealed to the UN for international help in his fight to protect his people from gold miners.

Please ask for the capture and prosecution of the criminals who killed my brothers and sisters. . . . The miners kill every living thing that stands in the way of their quest for gold.[49]

The miners, however, were never identified or arrested and gold prospecting continued unabated in Yanomami territory. It is estimated, in fact, that over 1 million gold miners remain in the Amazon today. Despite international outcry over the abuses and killings, miners continue to enter indigenous territories illegally. For the most part, the Brazilian government simply ignores their presence.

The Shining Path

During the latter part of the 1980s, another force threatened the indigenous communities: Peruvian guerrilla fighters who called themselves the Sendero Luminoso, or Shining Path. This Communist revolutionary group opposed both the elected government in Lima and other Latin American terrorist groups. When their own terrorist tactics failed to net large-scale support in

Peru's cities, Shining Path guerrillas began to recruit such Amerindian communities as the Ashaninka.

Initially viewed as benefactors when they entered the Amazon in 1987, the Shining Path quickly won over the leadership of the Ashaninka and other indigenous groups by promising the Amerindians better schools, medical facilities, and other improvements. The Amerindians, however, soon regretted the liaison. "By 1990," writes journalist Lawrence J. Speer, "Shining Path's courtship of the Ashaninka had degenerated into the predictable reign of terror that marked its campaigns throughout the war. Guerrillas murdered Ashaninka leaders, enslaved whole tribes, slaughtered the sick, and used native warriors as cannon fodder against the Peruvian Army."[50] In some estimates, the number of Ashaninka dead exceeded three thousand.

The Ashaninka people faced automatic weapons and other sophisticated arms with only a handful of shotguns to augment their bows and arrows and spears. As the guerrillas took control of traditional villages, thousands of indigenous people fled to more inaccessible areas of the jungle.

Was the Worst Over?

Ultimately, the Peruvian military defeated the guerrillas, and, in the early 1990s, the government stepped in to help the indigenous people. The Ashaninka replanted their fields and believed the worst of their problems were over. Their traditional way of life, however, was almost immediately endangered by a new threat.

At the urging of the Ecuadorian government, thousands of colonists began to move into the Ashaninka's ancestral land. As a result of this onslaught, many of the indigenous communities were systematically destroyed and their territories reduced in size. Ashaninka spokesman Rogelio Crus spoke of the problems to journalist Zoraida Portillo in 1999:

> They [the outsiders] don't know how to look after the land, they come, sow, harvest, burn, and on top of all this criticize us for being slack because we allow the soil to rest. Nothing grows here anymore, they burn entire hills of vegetation for one farm, in the end, they lose everything and move further in to continue the burning, and all on our ancestral lands.[51]

The government of Peru has, thus far, done little to protect the Ashaninka.

Although explorers, miners, colonists, and others have been coming into the Amazon for many centuries, only within the last fifty years have outsiders started to overuse the resources of the Amazon. The region continues to be raided for all sorts of goods including turtle oil, salted meat, mahogany, flavorings like vanilla and cacao, and plants for medicine. Oil drilling continues, as does gold mining and rubber tapping. With little concern for the effects these enterprises have on either the rain forest or the indigenous people, the exploitation of the Amazon is devastating the lives of Amerindians as it destroys their precious homelands.

Chapter 6

Threats to the Amazon and Its Inhabitants

The Amazon and its indigenous inhabitants have, over the course of the last fifty years, come under attack from many different sources. Pollution, destruction of the rain forest, and the indiscriminate killing of wildlife all pose a risk to the very fragile Amazon environment. These same factors also threaten the indigenous people, already shaken by disease, the loss of their homeland, and the extinction of many of their communities.

The Importance of the Rain Forest

The rain forest is an extremely fragile and complicated ecosystem in which every species, including humans, depends on each other for food and shelter. When one component of the forest is damaged, all other life is affected as well. Once an area of the forest is burned, for example, it takes over three hundred years for it to regenerate. Over the last twenty years, scientists estimate that the Amazon rain forest has been destroyed at the rate of thirteen thou-

sand acres a day, or about the equivalent of eight football fields per minute.

Westerners, for the most part, have always treated nature as something to control. Their view, according to representatives of the Rainforest Foundation, a group dedicated to the survival of the forest, "is that nature should be studied, dissected, and mastered . . . and that human progress is measured by the ability to extract natural resources and accumulate material wealth."[52] This attitude has led to the indiscriminate destruction and abuse of the rain forest.

The Amerindians, in contrast, believe that they are the trustees of the land and have a collective responsibility to preserve it for future generations. They have a deep respect for nature, a concept that is embodied in their spiritual and social lives. The Yanomami, for instance, believe that everything that nature creates is sacred. "They believe," write historians, "that their fate, and the fate of all people, is inescapably linked to the fate of their environment."[53]

Poor farmers resort to slash-and-burn techniques to create farmland. Such burning is one of many threats to the Amazon rain forest.

Threats to the Rain Forest

The governments of South America have, until very recently, shown very little interest in protecting the rain forest and its component ecosystems. This is due, in part, to the fact that most of the Amazon countries are very poor and face enormous economic and social problems. To them, the rain forest is a resource that has the potential of providing them with the needed profit they require to address their citizens' poverty and national economic problems.

The building of roads, farms, cattle ranches, and industrial complexes has already led to the destruction of thousands of acres of land. The forest has been cleared by burning, by the spraying of poisonous substances, and by huge, chain-dragging tractors. Without the tree cover to protect the land during the torrential seasonal rains, the cleared earth has been largely washed away, leaving the ground unable to support crops. Some of the damage done to the land and forest during the last forty years, scientists report, can never be undone.

Threats to the rain forest take many forms, the most severe being mining, pollution, logging, and the slash-and-burn activities that precede the transformation of forests into farmland. These activities have the potential to cause future catastrophes. "The predicted impact of this destruction," writes author David Yeadon, "is almost too dramatic to contemplate: violent climatic changes; vastly reduced oxygen production; increased carbon dioxide in the atmosphere; extinction of fragile indigenous

A barge floating on the Napo River in Ecuador passes road construction. The Amazon's vast rain forest is the victim of this kind of industrialization on a regular basis.

cultures; and elimination of vast untapped resources for food and medicine."[54]

Pollution

When the Europeans arrived in the Amazon five hundred years ago, they found millions of acres of unspoiled wilderness. This condition no longer exists in many places. Author Sy Montgomery visited many areas of the Amazon in the 1990s and reported that "the Amazon was full of trash. . . . We saw spray cans, cola bottles, oil cans every fifty yards or so [along the river.]"[55] Massive dynamiting along the river has also resulted in the deaths of numerous fish species, dolphins, and turtles, whose carcasses litter the rivers and shores of the Amazon.

The oil industry is one of the biggest contributors to the pollution of the region. To keep costs down, many of the big companies cut corners. Rather than properly disposing of toxic waste, for instance, they dump it into the streams and waters. As a result, water sources traditionally used by the Amerindian people are massively polluted by benzene and other deadly by-products of the oil industry.

Benzene can cause skin and nervous system disorders, as well as anemia, leukemia, and birth defects. "In large parts of Ecuador's jungle oil region," writes Mike Tidwell, "every man, woman, and child [is], in effect, taking a benzene bath each day by simply drinking, washing, or walking anywhere in the vicinity."[56]

Effects of Gold Mining

Gold miners have also had a devastating impact on both the environment and the in-digenous people who live in the Amazon. The constant flights of supply planes and the noise from generators and other equipment have frightened away many of the animals that the Amerindians rely on for food. High-pressure hoses have washed away many riverbanks and have also destroyed the spawning grounds of many indigenous fish.

One of the biggest dangers of mining, however, is mercury poisoning. Mercury is used to separate the gold from the soil and rocks of the Amazon. It is then dumped—nearly a thousand tons a year—back into the rivers where it wreaks havoc on the entire ecosystem.

The mercury poisons, not only the water, but the trees and animals, as well. In 1996, for instance, several species of fish had to be banned from human consumption because of high mercury levels. Many of the Amerindians, however, remain unaware of these bans and continue to eat the poisoned fish.

Mercury is extremely toxic and causes irreversible damage to the human nervous system. A neurotoxin, mercury enters the bloodstream when people eat the fish and causes a variety of neurological symptoms, brain damage, and birth defects. Consumption of mercury can be fatal, as well, and a large increase in child mortality rates in indigenous groups close to mining operations has been largely attributed to the presence of mercury in fish. "Studies have shown dangerously high and toxic levels of mercury," historian Marshall C. Eakin reports, "in the blood of peasants and Indians in [the] region."[57]

A South American gold miner uses mercury to separate soil from gold. Thousands of tons of toxic mercury are dumped into the Amazon every year.

Forced Relocation

In addition to the ecological disasters due to deforestation and the toxic effects of pollution, the Amerindians have been the victims of devastating diseases and forced relocation to other areas of the Amazon. During the nonindigenous pursuit of untapped natural resources and Amerindian land in the second half of the twentieth century, the construction of highways and dams, alone, resulted in the displacement of thousands of families and nearly wiped out a number of groups.

The Waimiri-Atroari of Brazil, for instance, now number less than eight hundred individuals. Their numbers were depleted in 1977 when they were forced to relocate because of the building of the Pan-American Highway, which runs from Alaska to the tip of South America. The Assurini are also on the brink of extinction. Their homeland was adversely affected by the building of a huge, hydroelectric dam.

In 1985, a development called Calha Norte drastically affected several different groups of indigenous people in Brazil. The project included a plan to set up roads and a chain of military barracks in the middle of the Macuxi Amerindians' homeland. The Brazilian army moved the Macuxi out by burning down their homes. The Yanomami also lost over half their land during this project.

Disease

The relatively recent threats from industry and development have been compounded by an old enemy, disease. Over the past twenty years, debilitating and fatal illnesses attributable to the presence and activity of gold prospectors, oil drillers, and road crews have killed thousands of Amerindians. The range of diseases, in fact, has grown dramatically as the rain forest has been cut down. "Host insects," writes Joe Kane, "once content to ply their business in the canopy have come in closer with human prey, and standing water trapped behind large new dams provides fertile breeding grounds [for disease-carrying insects.]"[58]

Once largely unaffected by malaria, a disease carried by mosquitoes, the indigenous people of the Amazon are now facing epidemics of that tropical disease. In some villages there are so many sick people that

A Yanomami shaman attempts to cure a child of malaria. The Yanomami have fallen prey to a malaria epidemic caused by the development of their lands.

there is no one left to perform the curing rituals. In 2000, for example, over three thousand Yanomami came down with malaria, according to statistics from Brazil's National Health Foundation.

Many Amerindians also suffer from river blindness, a disease spread by black flies. The disease causes sight-impairing sores around the eyes along with severe itching. While this disease is not fatal, it, nonetheless, often leads to blindness, leaving its victims unable to hunt, farm, or perform their normal activities. Other diseases such as tuberculosis, rabies, cholera, typhus, yellow fever, measles, and influenza have all taken their toll on indigenous populations. Children under the age of five account for almost half of all Amerindian deaths.

Compounding the problem of disease is the lack of health care for the indigenous populations of the Amazon. Adequate health care has been hampered by lack of money and the Amerindians' inaccessibility to the necessary services. Western medicines and doctors are often unavailable to the poor and to the Amerindians of the region.

Extinction

Disease, pollution, drastic changes in traditional ways of life, and premature death have all contributed to a decrease in Amerindian population figures. An estimated 250,000 indigenous people still inhabit the Amazon today. A complete and accurate count is made more difficult by the fact that many indigenous groups are classified in national censuses as "other." Journalist Kathyrn Therese Johnson elabo-

rates, noting that, in Venezuela, "the national census classifies persons as indigenous if they habitually speak a native language or if their way of life is so obviously aboriginal that they could not be classified [otherwise.]"[59] Many Amerindians, however, do not fit in these categories because they have either learned to speak Spanish or have adopted Western customs.

While an accurate population figure is difficult to obtain, anthropologists and other scientists do know that many indigenous groups have become extinct in the latter half of the twentieth century. Peruvian journalists report that between 1950 and 2000, "eleven ethnic groups have completely disappeared and another eighteen have officially been declared at risk of extinction."[60]

Author Sy Montgomery cites similar statistics for Brazil: "More than ninety Indian tribes in Brazil alone have become extinct since the turn of the century. . . . Murdered and enslaved, victims of foreign diseases, greed, religions, and alcohol, they are disappearing still."[61]

Anthropologists and other scientists hope that the remaining indigenous populations can be saved. Part of their optimism stems from their belief that there are probably yet uncontacted and unidentified groups deep in the jungle. *National Geographic* journalist W. Jesco Von Puttkamer agrees with this assessment: "Just when we . . . think we have found the last unknown tribe in the vast jungles of Brazil, someone poking into the wilderness will be greeted by a shower of arrows fired from some place hitherto believed to be uninhabited."[62]

Education

Throughout the Amazon, indigenous education systems are underfunded by South American governments. In many of the more isolated regions, if there are any teachers at all, they rarely have completed the sixth grade. Seldom, too, do teachers speak the indigenous languages.

Although education is free in many countries, thousands of indigenous children have no schools in their immediate area. Other children cannot take time out to go to school because their families need them to work in farms and fields. Other Amerindians do not want to educate their children in "white" schools because they do not believe that learning to read and write will put food on their tables.

There have, however, been a few success stories among the indigenous communities. According to a 2000 Peruvian report published in the *InterPress Service English News Wire:* "In response to a need for bilingual teachers in indigenous languages, Benito Contiricon, a native Ashaninka, has returned to the Peruvian jungle to teach his community's youth in their native language." Prior to that time, there were no Ashaninka teachers in the region.

The Shuar Federation of Ecuador has also recently begun to broadcast radio programming to various indigenous villages. These broadcasts not only keep the community informed about issues involving the Amerindians but serve to educate the listeners. Through radio and bilingual education programs, the Shuar can keep their children at home instead of sending them to boarding schools hundreds of miles away.

Adapting to Modern Society

As various external interests have moved into the Amazon, the Amerindians have been forced to adapt to many changing conditions. A few of the indigenous groups moved deeper into unexplored regions of the jungle and have, as a result, been able to preserve many of their traditional ways of life. The Ticuna of Brazil, for instance, have been able to retain their native language, rituals, cultural art forms, and traditional religion, while the Penare of western Guiana continue to live much as they did hundreds of years ago. These people are primarily hunters and gatherers who tend small gardens and live in familial huts made of palm thatch.

The majority of Amerindian people, however, have been more strongly affected by the presence of "outsiders" in the Amazon. While most indigenous people have maintained at least a part of their traditional way of life, they have, at the same time, become more Westernized. Many people, for instance, wear Western clothing and attend Christian churches. Other indigenous people have begun to look outside their villages for work, while still others, despairing over

Some indigenous peoples send their children to schools like the one pictured here. Most children, however, must remain at home to work with their families.

the changes that have occurred, have turned to self-destructive acts.

Degradation, Alcoholism, and Suicide

The Amazon is now attracting thousands of tourists who charter cruises along the river that visit many Amerindian villages. The indigenous people of the area, however, often find these visits extremely humiliating.

National Geographic journalist Carole DeVillers writes of her stay with the Wayana in Guiana:

> Here, increasing numbers of tourists regularly descend on the village's few families and behave like visitors

in a zoo. They bribe the bare-chested women to pose for pictures with them and pay men to do the same, brandishing hunting bows and arrows. . . . The effect on the Wayana is one of degradation, not merely in their own eyes, but in those of their children.[63]

Other groups of Amerindians have faced similar problems. They complain of feeling like slaves or animals and have learned over the years to dread tourist visits.

The degradation they experience as a result of insensitivity and rudeness by tourists and other outsiders has led many Amerindians to try to ease their pain in self-destructive ways. Alcoholism, in fact, has become epidemic in many indigenous communities.

The Amerindians, throughout their history, have consumed large quantities of *chicha*, the traditional beer, but alcohol abuse was extremely rare. When Westerners introduced stronger fermented beverages, the indigenous people liked the taste. When they used higher proof alcohol in the same way they had always used *chicha*, however, the more potent drinks had far different and more severe effects, leading to drunkenness, illness, and even death.

Some indigenous villages have banned the selling of alcohol by Westerners, but a brisk, often illegal, trade in liquor continues in spite of these efforts. Tourists driving along the roads in the Amazon now see what writer Tim Cahill calls a "familiar pattern. Indian people, wearing the ragged clothes of their conquerors, beg alongside the road . . . or simply stumble about in an alcoholic daze."[64]

Alcoholism only adds to the despair felt by many indigenous people. Feelings of hopelessness are increasingly leading

Adapting to Western Economies

During the latter half of the twentieth century, many indigenous people exposed to Western culture developed a desire for such Western items as clothing, food, tools, and alcohol. To acquire these items, however, the Amerindians, who had for their entire existence relied on a system of trade and exchange, were forced to enter the cash economies of South America. Simply put, they needed cash money to buy the goods they desired.

Thus, many Amerindians now work in factories, on farms, and on cattle ranches. Some join the army, while others work in the oil or rubber industry. A few of these jobs pay fairly well but most offer little monetary compensation. As a result, many indigenous communities are actively pursuing other ways to bring in money for their people. These methods include de-

veloping products to sell, making nurseries out of forest plants, and raising endangered animals for release into the wild.

A few Amerindian people have been criticized for the ways they have chosen to make money. The Kayapo of Brazil, for instance, have been accused of signing profitable logging and mining deals inside their protected homelands. Charges were made that the Kayapo, in doing so, were actually adding to the devastation and deforestation of the very land they should be protecting. Kayapo leaders have defended these actions by arguing that the money they make goes toward tribal health care and education, two areas the government has not addressed adequately. The Kayapo also point out that the money they receive is merely a small percentage of the profits made by the mining and logging companies.

Indigenous Aggression in the Twentieth Century

Several indigenous groups have continued to respond aggressively to missionaries and other outsiders. The Waorani, for example, came to the attention of the world in 1956 when the group killed five American missionaries who were attempting to establish contact with them. This group's history has always been characterized by violence, perpetrated both by and against them.

Another Amerindian group, the Tagaeri, also reacted violently to contact with outsiders. In July 1987, two Catholic missionaries attempted to convince them to allow oil company personnel to enter their territory. Both missionaries were killed, after which the Amerindians abandoned their homes and fled deeper into the rain forest.

When Carolyn Bennett Patterson rented a small motorboat on a visit to Xingu National Park in Brazil in the 1970s, she and her indigenous guide ran into trouble. She describes this encounter in her book *Of Lands, Legends, and Laughter:* "I had no sooner spotted a cluster of thatch-roofed huts atop a nearby rise when the huts seemed to burst open, loosing a stream of armed, naked men. With spine-chilling screams, hoots, and howls, they rushed down to the river, pausing only briefly to shoot arrows and throw long spears . . . in our direction." The guide gunned the motor and, as the boat sped away, he explained to Patterson that the mere presence of the motorboat had aroused the group's suspicion.

Amerindians to turn to the more devastating solution of suicide. In the Guarani community of Brazil, for instance, suicides have become nearly commonplace. On their dry, weed-infested reservation, these Amerindians are unable to live by their traditional methods of hunting and fishing. Religious practices have, for the most part, been abandoned and life has become nearly meaningless. Like thousands of other Amerindians, they have been reduced to begging in order to obtain food and other necessities of life. This breakdown of traditional life has resulted in the increased rates of suicide reported among indigenous groups.

Breakdown in Spiritual Practices

A significant breakdown in the traditional spirituality of the Amerindians has added to the problems they face in modern society. Many of these difficulties have been intensified by the continued presence of missionaries.

The actions of missionaries in indigenous communities have always been controversial. Supporters point out that, by teaching the Amerindians to read and write, missionaries are preparing indigenous groups for the future. These defenders also claim that, for decades, the missionaries were the only people to take a positive interest in the welfare of the Amerindians.

Critics, however, cite the heavy-handed approach of many outsiders who come in the name of religion. Author Joe Kane provides one example: "One American missionary had forced a hungry Ashaninka boy to sing *Nearer My God to Thee* [in English], before permitting him to eat."[65] Other missionaries have forbidden the Amerindians to practice their traditional forms of religion, often by punishing the community or by withholding food and other supplies.

Many of the indigenous people have learned to compromise despite these kinds of attitudes. They attend Christian churches while, at the same time, retaining many of their traditional practices and beliefs. Their world continues to include forest spirits and village shamans with supernatural powers.

Despite the many problems facing the Amerindians in modern South American society, the indigenous people of the Amazon continue their struggle to overcome the odds. Holding onto some of their spiritual practices and traditional ways of life, the indigenous communities are beginning to find ways to fight back so that they will have a say in their future.

Chapter 7

Hope for the Future

Facing the destruction of their homeland and the extinction of their people, today the Amerindians of the Amazon are fighting back. Finding new ways to support themselves, forming protest groups, and joining with worldwide conservation efforts, the indigenous people, for the first time in their modern history, are making their voices heard. In the last twenty years, they have made steady progress toward their goals of saving the rain forest and having a role in their own future.

Returning to Traditional Skills

While hundreds of indigenous people have found employment with multinational and South American industries, farms, and ranches, they have discovered that these jobs are hard to obtain and offer little monetary incentive. As a result, many Amerindians have returned to traditional crafts and skills as a way to support themselves and their communities.

The Wayana of French Guiana, for instance, have developed a very ambitious handicraft program. Called *Culture Artisat Wayana*, this craft-producing cooperative assists the Wayana to sell their crafts in different towns along the Amazon River. The Amerindians produce a variety of items, including necklaces, bracelets, baskets, bows and arrows, and pottery. The different crafts are then taken to the cooperative where they are sold to tourists, other indigenous villages, and the city dwellers of South America.

The Guahibo of Venezuela also make a variety of items. Indigenous women make dolls from bark and fiber and then decorate them with colored seeds. These handmade dolls feature dresses of pounded bark or loose woven fibers. Around ten inches tall, the dolls have a string on their heads so that little girls can hang them up with other family belongings.

The Piaroa of Venezuela are noted for their traditional costumes and masks, all made with natural fibers, bark, reed, and colored vegetable dyes. The faces of the masks are formed with beeswax and then painted, while the costumes are decorated with paintings that depict various mythological creatures.

The Piapoco of Colombia are relearning an ancient skill and are, today, noted for their carvings of animals such as the eagle and armadillo. These carvings are made from lightweight balsa wood and shaped using only machetes and knives. Another item that has become increasingly popular with tourists is the rainstick, a hollow tube filled with seeds into which nails are pounded. When the tube is turned on its end, the sound of seeds striking nails as they tumble down is similar to that of falling rain.

Basket Making

Many Amerindian communities are also returning to traditional basket making to earn much needed income. The Yekuana of Venezuela are among the many indigenous people noted for this skill. They weave intricate geometric designs and images of animals into their baskets using a variety of natural dyes to create different colors. One of their baskets, the *wuwu*, is bell-shaped and designed to fit snugly into the small of

A band of local Indians takes part in a political demonstration in Brazil's capital city. Indigenous peoples have made steady political progress in recent years.

A Yanomami woman weaves a basket in the traditional manner. Native arts and crafts are still practiced as a livelihood in the Amazon basin.

a woman's back for the purpose of carrying fruit and grain. Yekuana men craft tray baskets that they present to the women they are interested in marrying.

The Warao of Venezuela are also known for their beautiful baskets. The entire family plays a role in the weaving process with the men gathering seeds from marshy areas while the younger children sort through them, grouping them by the seeds' sizes. While women do the actual weaving, older members of the family assist in the dyeing process. These baskets have become very popular with tourists who come from all over South America and the world to obtain them.

Ecotourism

Ecotourism is another new, economic venture for the Amerindians. This practice, in fact, has become popular worldwide within the last twenty years as a result of increased public awareness about the various dangers facing wilderness areas. "Most ecotours have as their objective," writes author Mike Tidwell, "more than just taking travelers to see pretty things in hard to reach places. . . . The point is to educate

Sting and the Rainforest Foundation

Since the mid-1980s, many internationally recognized celebrities, including actor Richard Gere and the late singer–songwriter John Denver, have spoken out against the exploitation of the Amazon and its indigenous people. One of the most outspoken of these celebrities has been rock star Sting.

Sting journeyed to the Amazon in the spring of 1989 and, during his stay there, visited the Kayapo Amerindians and met their leader, Chief Raoni. The musician learned that the Kayapo were being killed and pushed off their traditional homelands by gold miners and loggers. In May 1989, he called a press conference to tell the world about the struggles of this indigenous group.

Later that same year, Sting and his wife, actress Trude Styler, founded the Rainforest Foundation, a nonprofit organization dedicated to the preservation of the Amazon rain forest and the Kayapo Amerindians. The foundation, since that time, has supported indigenous people around the world while also attempting to protect the rain-forest habitats where they live.

In 1993, the Brazilian government responded to pressure from the Rainforest Foundation and other groups and announced the creation of a special reserve in the Amazon where the Kayapo could live undisturbed by outsiders. Despite the creation of this reserve, the Kayapo continue to be exploited by outsiders.

along the way."[66] The education comes in the form of teaching travelers to appreciate wildlife, wilderness areas, and the many benefits of saving natural environments for future generations.

Many indigenous groups are welcoming ecotourism in order to bring much needed income into their communities. By promoting this kind of travel, the Amerindians are also helping to protect the environment and their homelands. Furthermore, the Amerindians hope that some of the money derived from this practice will be used to fund wilderness parks and preserves in South America. In fact, many indigenous groups see ecotourism as one of the few ways left for them to save the rain forest.

The National Indian Foundation

One of the problems that the indigenous people are now focusing on is the failure of South American governments to follow through with their promises of protection. The Indian Protection Service of Brazil was created in 1910 for this purpose, while

Celebrities such as Sting (first row, second from right) have helped publicize the plight of the Amazon rain forest and its indigenous peoples.

various laws were passed that supposedly guaranteed indigenous people a right to live in their traditional homelands. Never living up to expectations, the service had, by the 1960s, become corrupt and was replaced by the National Indian Foundation of Brazil, known by its Portuguese acronym FUNAI.

FUNAI was created to help mediate conflicts that arose between the indigenous people of Brazil and various outside interests. The organization was also charged with improving the health of the Amerindians and defining the boundaries of their lands. Despite these lofty goals, the organization's leaders have had, in the opinion of historian Marshall C. Eakin, quite a different intent. He says that FUNAI's true objective is "to integrate Indians into national life and guarantee that they do not stand in the way of efforts to develop the Amazon."[67]

Critics of the National Indian Foundation have made widespread claims of corruptness and ineptness. For one thing, the agency lacks any kind of enforcement branch. While the organization can call on the federal police to protect the indigenous people and their land, this rarely happens. In fact, the foundation itself has been implicated in the killing of Amerindians by dynamite, machine guns, and sugar laced with arsenic.

In the 1970s, for example, the National Indian Foundation told the Wasusus that they had to move off their reservation to a new home on the savanna, an area of grassland on the edge of the rain forest that was completely inadequate for their needs. The Wasusus, a farming people, found the soil poor, the game scarce, and the climate cold. They had been relocated to make room for timber enterprises that had been commissioned by the Brazilian government to cut down thousands of trees. Only after several world organizations, including the National Geographic Society and the Smithsonian Institution, became influential advocates were the Wasusus allowed to return to their homeland.

Indigenous Protests

Receiving little if any support from the so-called Indian protection agencies or the governments of South America, the indigenous people of the Amazon began acting and speaking out on their own behalf. With growing worldwide interest in the environment and the rain forest, the Amerindians found a ready-made audience for their grievances.

In February 1989, the Kayapo of Brazil, with the assistance of rock star Sting, called a meeting of the indigenous people of the Amazon and invited the world press to attend. This gathering was held so that the Amerindians could protest the building of six large dams that threatened to destroy their homelands along the Xingu River. The Kayapo and other indigenous leaders hoped their efforts would halt the dam projects. Over five hundred indigenous people arrived at the meeting wearing traditional costumes and singing war songs. Soon after the meeting and, as a result of worldwide protest, the World Bank, an organization

The Cofan Survival Fund

The Cofan of Ecuador have been in the forefront of world attention during the last twenty years due to their efforts to protect their homelands against oil developers. The Cofan Survival Fund was established in 1998 to help with these efforts and to also carry out conservation and community development projects. The organization's primary goal has been to bolster the Cofan economy and preserve Cofan traditions. According to the organization's newsletter: "Much of our recent effort has gone toward protecting our ancestral lands, getting titles and treaties that ensure the proper use and management of . . . resources."

The Cofan are also involved in identifying species of animals that have been endangered by the destruction of the rain forest. One such project led to the successful release of over twenty-five thousand turtles back into the environment. The Cofan are now working to save the caiman, a small alligator found in the Amazon.

The Cofan Survival Fund is currently sponsoring many indigenous people to attend better schools in Quito, Ecuador. There, the young are learning to speak not only Cofan, but English, Spanish, and French as well. The hope is that these individuals will return to the Cofan community and provide well-educated leaders who can continue the group's efforts to preserve their homeland.

that had been funding the project, called off its financial contributions, effectively shutting down the dam building.

Three years later, in 1992, hundreds of Amazonian indigenous people traveled to the Earth Summit held in Rio de Janeiro, Brazil. Once again, the Amerindians protested the destruction of their homelands and told journalists about the plight of their communities. And, in February 2001, over four thousand members of various Ecuadorian-Amerindian groups camped out at Salesian University in that country's capital city of Quito. The indigenous people marched on the Ecuadorian Congress in a visible show of force, protesting against government eco-

nomic measures that would have negatively impacted the Amerindians. They were partially successful in preventing farming and ranching legislation that would have reduced and destroyed much of their homeland.

Today, many indigenous groups are at the vanguard of antigovernment protests in South America. In an interview with journalist Alistair Scrutton, Amerindian Benica Malaver stated: "The government has always seen us as animals, nothing more. We want our language, culture protected."[68]

The Shuar Federation

The Shuar of Ecuador were one of the first indigenous communities to form an organization to speak out on their own behalf. In 1964, they announced the creation of the Shuar Federation, a nonprofit group that represented over twenty thousand people from many different Shuar communities.

Supported by a group of Catholic missionaries, the organization emerged as a response to certain agricultural reform laws introduced by Ecuadorian dictator Rodriguez Lara. In 1964, Lara began to encourage colonization of a part of the Ama-zon that had, for centuries, been the traditional home of the Shuar people. "When the farming and oil industries moved into the area," wrote federation representatives at the time, "the ecological effects were devastating. The Indians' lifestyle was interrupted and their lands were threatened."[69]

In spite of constant harassment from colonists and government representatives, this organization has achieved many of its goals, including the legal recognition of

Dressed in traditional ceremonial garb, this Indian votes in Brazil's 2002 presidential election. Indians of the Amazon have come to understand the power of collective political action.

Shuar lands and a radio school system that reaches children in remote areas.

Other Indigenous Organizations

The Coordinating Body for the Indigenous Peoples' Organization of the Amazon Basin (COICA) was formed in 1984. This group represents thousands of indigenous communities in the countries of Brazil, Ecuador, Bolivia, Peru, and Colombia. Among many notable achievements, COICA has been responsible for the founding of the Amazon Indigenous University, a college devoted to the preservation of Amerindian languages.

In 1993, the representatives of nineteen Venezuelan Amerindian groups held the first Congress of Indigenous Peoples of the Amazon. This meeting resulted in the formation of the Organizacion Regional de Pueblos Indigenas de Amazonas, a group committed to protecting and promoting the interests of the indigenous people of the Amazon.

Despite protests from this organization and others, however, the Venezuelan government in 1997 voted into law Decree 1850, which opened up nearly half of the Imataca Forest Reserve to industry, mining, and logging. Since that time, the Amerindians, claiming ancestral rights to the land, have clashed repeatedly with miners and developers. In 1998, the Pemon Amerindians set up roadblocks in protest, but their simple and traditional weapons were no match for the rubber bullets and tear gas used by military forces.

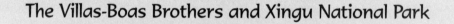

The Villas-Boas Brothers and Xingu National Park

In 1961, three Brazilian-born brothers —Orlando, Claudio, and Leonardo Villas-Boas—persuaded the Brazilian government to create a national park along the Xingu River. Impressed by indigenous life and culture, the brothers fought for the rights of the Amerindians, while, at the same time, living with the various communities for many years. They hoped the park would protect the indigenous people from disease and other Western influences that were destroying traditional ways of life.

The brothers' efforts culminated in the creation of Xingu National Park, an area that they were able to keep free of outsiders only briefly. The Brazilian government's pledge to limit use of the area to the indigenous people was broken in 1971, when highway builders moved in. A few years later, all three brothers were dead, but the Amerindians took over the fight to keep their homelands. While they have had a few successes, for the most part, the Brazilian government has ignored their rights and allowed various outside interests to move into the area.

Improvements in Health Care

During the last twenty-five years, several South American countries have taken steps toward improving the health status of its indigenous people. In the mid-1980s, for instance, the Committee for the Creation of the Yanomami Park in Brazil provided the Yanomami with doctors and various vaccination programs. This effort was initially very successful in decreasing the number of indigenous deaths.

Problems developed, however, in August 1987, when gold miners invaded Yanomami land. FUNAI, an organization responsible for protecting the Amerindians, was ordered by the Brazilian government to remove the health care workers. Government officials never fully explained their decision but alluded to a lack of funds to continue caring for the indigenous people.

For years afterward, the Yanomami had no health workers and suffered dramatic increases in disease rates. In 2000, however, Brazil spent $6 million to again provide health care to the Yanomami. This new program pays for over two hundred health workers who have been commissioned to work full-time with the Yanomami. The workers must sometimes hike for days into jungle highlands to reach the more isolated villages.

In 1996, aid from Great Britain helped the country of Colombia to build a hospital for the exclusive use of the Amerindian population. And in Peru, a health care project has shown great promise of bridging the gap between traditional and Western medicine. Shipibo shamans have been training Peruvian health care workers by running workshops that teach ways to integrate the two kinds of health care.

Many European countries and organizations such as Survival International are also giving direct help to the people of the Amazon. Aid from the United States, for example, is being spent on projects that, among other things, help the indigenous people to sell their agricultural products and their traditional handicrafts. International conservation organizations such as the World Wildlife Fund have also been at the forefront in alerting the world to the plight of the rain forest and the indigenous people who live there.

Indigenous Politicians Speak Out

The indigenous people of the Amazon are also beginning to take an active role in politics. Prior to 1988 in Brazil, all Amerindians, regardless of age, were considered minors and wards of the state. They could not vote or make any decisions for themselves, even about issues that affected them. The situation began to change for the better in 1988, though, when the indigenous population of Brazil was given full citizenship in Brazil.

During the last decade of the twentieth century, a number of indigenous leaders decided to run for government office. Mario Juruna, a Xavante chief, was elected to the Brazilian Congress and, during his short term in office, often appeared in public and at congressional hearings in traditional indigenous attire and body paint.

Ailton Krenak, a Krenak Amerindian, was named the national coordinator of all Brazilian indigenous groups in the 1990s. Krenak was instrumental in creating an alliance between rubber tappers and the indigenous population that eventually evolved into an organization called the Forest People's Alliance. Krenak also served on the National Council on the Environment and was able to vote on a number of important issues affecting the Amerindians of the Brazilian Amazon.

The Forest People's Alliance, a coalition group made up of rubber tappers and indigenous people, has developed many different strategies to protect the rain forest. The organization has, for example, called on South American countries to halt the building of roads, dams, and mining projects. The alliance has also been instrumental in stopping the resettlement of many indigenous groups in the Amazon. It is now advocating a stronger role for Amerindians in decision making on those issues that affect the rain forest, while, at the same time, teaching Hispanic South American settlers to live on the land without destroying it.

In October 2002, Ecuador's indigenous movement won more than 12 percent of the vote in that country's general elections.

"Through their struggle," writes journalist Kintto Lucas, "the [indigenous] communities have gradually won spaces in the country's public life, and now have an important presence in the political agenda."[70]

The Future

During the last fifteen years, there have been a number of indications that better times are ahead for both the Amerindians of the Amazon and their rain-forest homeland. The Shuar Federation in Ecuador, for instance, has been able to survey, map, and obtain title rights to nearly four hundred small indigenous communities. Other groups, however, have had only limited success in regaining ancestral land. In Venezuela, for instance, fewer than 30 percent of indigenous communities hold documents giving them legal title to the land they have traditionally occupied. With increased national representation and the help of indigenous and international groups, however, the Amerindians hope to increase these numbers in the twenty-first century.

Many areas of the rain forest are being replanted. PetroBras, the national oil and gas company of Brazil, has set up a seed bank and has promised to plant over twenty thousand new trees every year on many of their oil sites. Other companies are beginning to follow their example by enacting prohibitions against the release of toxic substances into the environment. Many South American governments have, in fact, closed several factories that were disobeying environmental laws. National parks and reserves, many of which are being controlled

A native Amazonian boy poses for a photo. Despite continued development of the Amazon, most tribes are working to preserve their traditions and to control their own future.

and protected by Amerindian groups, have been created throughout the Amazon.

Problems, however, remain. Kayapo chief Raoni was speaking for the Amerindians in the late 1980s when he told Sting: "Every year, the burning of the forest by the white settler gets closer and closer [to unex-plored regions and untouched areas of the Amazon]. You must help me stop it or there will be no forest left."[71]

The days of isolation for the indigenous people of the Amazon are over. "Given the enormous reach of modern communication technology and given the pressures by those favoring development," writes historian Marshall C. Eakin, "the option of isolation has disappeared. The best the Indians can hope for is to strike a bargain with outsiders to maintain as much of their traditions as possible."[72]

The Amerindians of the Amazon are today demanding the right to choose their own future and to control their own destiny. Ashaninka leader Santiago Contiricon sums up the position held by many indigenous groups: "We want to assimilate with the national economy and achieve a level of development that ensures the well-being of our people, but we do not want to stop being Ashaninka."[73]

Notes

Introduction: The Amazon and Its Inhabitants

1. Marshall C. Eakin, *Brazil: The Once and Future Country*. New York: St. Martin's, 1997, p. 87.

2. Loren McIntyre, *Amazonia*. San Francisco: Sierra Club, 1991, p. xiii.

Chapter 1: Adapting to Life in the Amazon

3. Quoted in Sy Montgomery, *Journey of the Pink Dolphins*. New York: Simon and Schuster, 2000, p. 107.

4. Alvin M. Josephy Jr., *America in 1492*. New York: Knopf, 1992, p. 185.

5. Carolyn Bennett Patterson, *Of Lands, Legends, and Laughter*. Golden, CO: Fulcrum, 1998, p. 83.

6. Joe Kane, *Running the Amazon*. New York: Knopf, 1989, p. 161.

7. "Kayapos," *Culture* http://lex.n.chs. north-battleford.sk.ca.

8. Josephy, *America in 1492*, p. 187.

9. Manuel Lucena Salmoral, *America in 1492: Portrait of a Continent Five Hundred Years Ago*. New York: Facts On File, 1990, p. 38.

10. Mike Tidwell, *Amazon Stranger*. Guilford, CT: Lyons, 1996, p. 67.

11. Josephy, *America in 1492*, p. 187.

Chapter 2: Amerindian Society and Culture

12. Josephy, *America in 1492*, p. 199.

13. Josephy, *America in 1492*, p. 192.

14. "Native American Indian Cultures," Native American Indian Cultures. http://indian-cultures.com.

15. Carole DeVillers, "What Future for the Wayana Indians?" *National Geographic*, January 1983, p. 82.

16. Patterson, *Of Lands, Legends, and Laughter*, p. 87.

17. Puruna Mucushiwa, "Chicha and the Zaparo Festival," *Indigenous Culture in Ecuador*, Ecuador Explorer. www. ecua dorexplorer.com.

18. Quoted in Michael Wood, *Conquistadors*. Berkeley and Los Angeles: University of California Press, 2000, p. 221.

19. Tidwell, *Amazon Stranger*, p. 195.

20. Kathyrn Therese Johnson, "Venezuela: Contemporary Social Stratification," *Countries of the World*, January 1, 1991, eLibrary. www.elibrary.com.

Chapter 3: Religion, Spirituality, and War

21. Michael Harner, *The Way of the Shaman*. San Francisco: HarperCollins, 1980, p. xvii.

22. Montgomery, *Journey of the Pink Dolphins*, p. 135.

23. Quoted in Elisabet Sahtouris, "Shuar," *Shuar, Life Web*: Shuar. www.ratical.org.

24. Salmoral, *America in 1492*, p. 64.

25. Quoted in Sahtouris, "Shuar."

26. DeVillers, "What Future for the Wayana Indians?" p. 77.

27. Harner, *The Way of the Shaman*, p. 17.

28. "Kayapos."

29. Josephy, *America in 1492*, p. 312.

30. "Ritual Mortar," Orinoco Online. www.orinoco.org.

31. Maria Magdelena Kayap, "The Tsantza Celebration," *"Shrinking Heads: The Shuar Indigenous People of Ecuador.* Ecuador Explorer. www.ecuadorexplorer.com.

32. "Head Shrinking and the Purpose of Tsanta," *The History of the Shuar, Head Hunter.* www.head-hunter.com

Chapter 4: Europeans Discover the Amazon

33. Project Amazonas, "A Brief History of the History of Amazon Exploration," *The History of Amazon Exploration,* Project Amazonas. www.projectamazonas.com.

34. Quoted in Eakin, *Brazil*, p. 90.

35. Time-Life Editors, *The Search for El Dorado.* Alexandria, VA: Time-Life Books, 1994, p. 14.

36. Kane, *Running the Amazon*, p. 161.

37. Tim Cahill, *Road Fever*. New York: Vintage, 1991, p. 81.

Chapter 5: Opening Up the Amazon

38. Eakin, *Brazil*, p. 90.

39. Montgomery, *Journey of the Pink Dolphins*, p. 37.

40. McIntyre, *Amazonia*, p. 37.

41. Cahill, *Road Fever*, p. 81.

42. Eakin, *Brazil*, p. 95.

43. Montgomery, *Journey of the Pink Dolphins*, p. 159.

44. Michael S. Serrill, "Brazil: Something Terrible Happened," *Time International*, September 6, 1993, eLibrary. www. elibrary.com.

45. Quoted in DeVillers, "What Future for the Wayana?" p. 69.

46. Quoted in Bruce Northam and Brad Olsen, *In Search of Adventure.* San Francisco: Consortium of Collective Consciousness, 1999, p.302.

47. Serrill, "Brazil: Something Terrible Happened."

48. Quoted in Valerie Taliman, "Yanomami Slaughtered for Gold," *Circle*, September 1, 1993, eLibrary. www.elibrary.com

49. Quoted in Taliman, "Yanomami Slaughtered for Gold."

50. Lawrence J. Speer, "Devastated by Peru's Shining Path," *Washington Times*, January 23, 1995, eLibrary. www.elibrary.com.

51. Quoted in Zoraida Portillo, "Population—Peru: Colonization Threatens the Indigenous Ashaninka," *InterPress Service English News Wire*, January 23, 1999.

Chapter 6: Threats to the Amazon and Its Inhabitants

52. "Indigenous Peoples," The Rainforest Foundation UK. www.rainforestfoundationuk.org.

53. "About the Yanomami," Amanaka'a Amazon Network. www.amanakaa.org.

54. David Yeadon, *The Way of the Wanderer*. San Francisco: Traveler's Tales, 2001, p. 222.

55. Montgomery, *Journey of the Pink Dolphins*, p. 42.

56. Tidwell, *Amazon Stranger*, p. 156.

57. Eakin, *Brazil*, p. 249.

58. Kane, *Running the Amazon*, p. 257.

59. Johnson, "Venezuela: Contemporary Social Stratification."

60. "Development—Peru: Indians Want Modernity Without Losing Identity," *InterPress Service English News Wire*, March 3, 2000.

61. Montgomery, *Journey of the Pink Dolphins*, p. 299.

62. W. Jesco Von Puttkamer, "Stone Age Present Meets Stone Age Past," *National Geographic*, January 1979, p. 863.

63. DeVillers, "What Future for the Wayana Indians?" p. 80.

64. Cahill, *Road Fever*, p. 81.

65. Kane, *Running the Amazon*, p. 191.

Chapter 7: Hope for the Future

66. Tidwell, *Amazon Stranger*, p. 9.

67. Eakin, *Brazil*, p. 96.

68. Quoted in Alistair Scrutton, "Indians' Protest in Ecuador Shows Political Muscle," *Reuters*, February 7, 2001.

69. "Shuar Federation," Shuar Federation. www2.truman.edu

70. Kintto Lucas, "Amazon Natives Struggle to Survive," *InterPress Service English News Wire*, July 2, 2001.

71. Quoted in Sting, "Beginnings," The Rainforest Foundation UK. www.rainforestfoundaitonuk.org.

72. Eakin, *Brazil*, p. 122.

73. Quoted in "Development—Peru: Indians Want Modernity Without Losing Identity."

For Further Reading

Books

Cousteau Society, *An Adventure in the Amazon*. New York: Simon and Schuster, 1991. This book follows explorer, journalist, and documentary filmmaker Yves Jacques Cousteau and his team as they travel the Amazon. The book includes glimpses of the Amazon and the Amerindians who live there.

Ann Heinrichs, *Brazil*. New York: Childrens Press, 1997. This book gives an overall picture of Brazil and contains an excellent section on the Amazon and its inhabitants.

Anna Lewington, *Rainforest Amerindians*. Austin, TX: Raintree Steck–Vaughn, 1993. This outstanding book focuses on many of the different Amerindians who live in the Amazon River basin.

Peter Lourie, *Amazon*. Honesdale, PA: Caroline House, 1991. A look at the Amazon and its inhabitants.

Marion Morrison, *Ecuador*. New York: Childrens Press, 2000. An overall look at the country of Ecuador and the indigenous people of that region.

Michael Pollard, *The Amazon*. New York: Marshall Cavendish, 1998. An excellent book about the Amazon and its inhabitants.

Julia Waterlow, *The Amazon*. Austin, TX: Raintree Steck–Vaughn, 1994. An excellent look at the Amazon and its inhabitants.

Jane Kohen Winter and Kitt Baguley, *Venezuela*. New York: Marshall Cavendish, 2002. An overall look at the country of Venezuela, the Amazon, and the indigenous people of that region.

Websites

"Native American Indian Cultures," Native American Indian Cultures. http://indian-cultures.com. This excellent site leads to information on nearly three dozen different indigenous groups of the Amazon.

Cesar Payaguaje. "I am Going to Tell You About How the Canoe Came to Be," *Build a Dugout Canoe—Amazon Ecuador*, Ecuador Explorer. www.ecuadorexplorer.com. The author, a Secoya Amerindian, relates the legend behind the canoe and its actual construction.

"Yanomami Indians," *Yanomami Indians*. Crystal Links. www.crystalinks.com. This Internet website offers a good background on the Yanomami Indians of Brazil and Venezuela.

Works Consulted

Books

Tim Cahill, *Road Fever*. New York: Vintage, 1991. A contributing editor for *Outside* magazine, the author embarks on a trip down the Pan-American Highway, which runs from Alaska to the tip of South America. The book contains several references to the Amazon, its inhabitants, and the problems facing the region today.

Marshall C. Eakin, *Brazil: The Once and Future Country*. New York: St. Martin's, 1997. An excellent history of Brazil that includes good sections on the Amazon and the indigenous people who live there.

Michael Harner, *The Way of the Shaman*. San Francisco: HarperCollins, 1980. Harner has practiced shamanism and shamanic healing for many years. This book describes, among other things, the author's visit with the Jivaro of Peru and their shamanic techniques.

Alvin M. Josephy Jr., *America in 1492*. New York: Knopf, 1992. An excellent book about the world of the Amerindians before the arrival of Christopher Columbus in 1492, including a very good chapter on the indigenous people of the Amazon.

Joe Kane, *Running the Amazon*. New York: Knopf, 1989. An account of the author's 1985 journey along the full length of the Amazon. He describes the area in detail along with his encounters with the Amerindians he and his party met along the way.

Doug Lanksy, *Up the Amazon Without a Paddle*. New York: Meadowbrook, 1999. This book contains a series of essays, one of which is about the author's experiences in the Amazon where he is taught to hunt with the blowgun by a group of Amerindians.

Loren McIntyre, *Amazonia*. San Francisco: Sierra Club, 1991. A photojournalist recounts his travels throughout the Amazon basin, accompanying text with abundant color photographs.

Sy Montgomery. *Journey of the Pink Dolphins*. New York: Simon and Schuster, 2000. This book is about the author's quest to find the pink river dolphins of the Amazon. She describes the dolphin and her encounters with the indigenous people of the area.

National Geographic Editors, *Emerald Realm: Earth's Precious Rain Forests*. Washington, DC: National Geographic Books, 1990. This excellent book focuses on the world's rain forests and offers a plethora of information about the Amazon and its inhabitants.

————, *Primitive Worlds*. Washington, DC: National Geographic Books, 1973. One chapter of this book focuses on the Yanomami of Venezuela.

David Noland, *Travels Along the Edge*. New York: Vintage, 1997. The author, a frequent contributor to *Outside* magazine, specializes in adventure travel. In this book he describes a number of trips to far-away places including one to the Amazon and a village of Yanomami Amerindians.

Bruce Northam and Brad Olsen, *In Search of Adventure*. San Francisco: Consortium of Collective Consciousness, 1999. This book contains a series of essays, one of which features a visit to the Cofan of Ecuador and their continuing struggle to fight oil interests in their territory.

Carolyn Bennett Patterson, *Of Lands, Legends, and Laughter*. Golden, CO: Fulcrum, 1998. The author was the first woman editor of *National Geographic* magazine. In this book she describes some of her journeys for that magazine, including a trip to Brazil to write about the Txukahamei.

Manuel Lucena Salmoral, *America in 1492: Portrait of a Continent Five Hundred Years Ago*. New York: Facts On File, 1990. The author looks at North and South American indigenous groups at the time of Christopher Columbus's arrival in 1492. There is a good section about the Amazon area and its inhabitants.

George E. Stuart, *Ancient Pioneers: The First Americans*. Washington, DC: National Geographic Books, 2001. An excellent book that describes archaeological evidence of the original inhabitants throughout the Americas. The book includes a section describing some of the indigenous people of the Amazon.

Mike Tidwell, *Amazon Stranger*. Guilford, CT: Lyons, 1996. The author spent many months with the Cofan Amerindians of Ecuador and their chief Randy Borman, as the indigenous people fought to save their land from big oil interests in that region of the Amazon.

Time-Life Editors, *The Search for El Dorado*. Alexandria, VA: Time-Life Books, 1994. This book offers a good section on Spaniard Francisco de Orellana's journey on the Amazon and the Spanish search for El Dorado.

Michael Wood. *Conquistadors*. Berkeley and Los Angeles: University of California Press, 2000. In this excellent book, the author follows the trails and footsteps of the Spanish conquistadors in the Americas. There is an excellent chapter on Spaniard Francisco de Orellana's journey down the Amazon.

David Yeadon. *The Way of the Wanderer*. San Francisco: Traveler's Tales, 2001. A series of essays describing the author's travels around the world, including a good one on the Amazon rain forest.

Periodicals

"Amazon Indians Urge Protection Against Exploitation," *Kyodo World News Service*, May 17, 2000.

Marcelo Ballve, "Disease Threaten Brazilian Tribe," *AP Online*, February 4, 2001.

Anthony Boadle, "Amazon Indians Meet to Save Rainforest Habitat," *Reuters*, May 21, 1997.

"Brazil to Remove Gold Prospectors from Amazon Indian Lands," *Kyodo World News Service*, February 16, 2001.

Napoleon A. Chagnon, "Yanomamo, the True People," *National Geographic*, August 1976.

"Development—Peru: Indians Want Modernity Without Losing Identity," *InterPress Service English News Wire*, March 3, 2000.

Carole DeVillers, "What Future for the Wayana Indians?" *National Geographic*, January 1983.

Joelle Diderich, "Yanomami Shamans Try to Halt Amazon Forest Fires," *Reuters*, March 19, 1998.

Andrea Dorfman, "Assault in the Amazon Brazil," *Time*, November 5, 1990.

Kintto Lucas, "Amazon Natives Struggle to Survive," *InterPress Service English News Wire*, July 2, 2001.

William B. Mitchell, "Guyana: Ethnic Groups and Languages," *Countries of the World*, January 1, 1991.

Zoraida Portillo, "Population—Peru: Colonization Threatens the Indigenous Ashaninka," *InterPress Service English News Wire*, January 23, 1999.

Alistair Scrutton, "Indians' Protest in Ecuador Shows Political Muscle," *Reuters*, February 7, 2001.

David Stoll, "Science Attacks Amazon Tribe," *New Republic,* March 19, 2001.

W. Jesco Von Puttkamer, "Stone Age Present Meets Stone Age Past," *National Geographic*, January 1979.

Internet Sources

"About the Yagua Indians," About the Yagua Indians. www.earth watch.org.

"About the Yanomami," Amanaka'a Amazon Network. www. amanakaa.org.

"An Introduction to Warao Music and Culture," Warao Indians of Venezuela. http://otto.cmr.fsu.edu.

"Ashaninka: The Rebirth of a Nation," *Rumbos Online*. www.rum bosperu.com.

Randall B. Borman, "The Cofan," Cofan: Guardians of the Rain Forest. www.cofan.org

"Head Shrinking and the Purpose of Tsanta," *The History of the Shuar, Head Hunter.* www.head-hunter.com.

Ray Howgego, "Francisco de Orellana," Discovers Web. www. win/tue.nl.

"Indigenous Peoples," The Rainforest Foundation UK. www.rainforest foundationuk.org.

"Introduction to the Jivaro Indian," The Jivaro Indians. www.head-hunter.com.

Maria Magdelena Kayap, "The Tsantza Celebration," *Shrinking Heads: The Shuar Indigenous People of Ecuador.* Ecuador Explorer. www.ecuadorexplorer.com.

Kathyrn Therese Johnson, "Venezuela: Contemporary Social Stratification," *Countries of the World*, January 1, 1991, eLibrary. www. elibrary.com.

"Kayapos," *Culture.* http://lex.nbchs.north-battleford.sk.ca.

Colin McEwan, "Seats of Power in the Tropical Forest Cultures of the Amazon," Fathom. www.fathom.com

Puruna Mucushiwa, "Chicha and the Zaparo Festival," *Indigenous Culture in Ecuador*, Ecuador Explorer. www.ecuadorexplorer.com.

"Native American Indian Cultures," Native American Indian Cultures. http://indian-cultures.com.

"Omaguan," Omagua. http://emuseum.mnsu.edu.

Project Amazonas, "A Brief History of the History of Amazon Exploration," *The History of Amazon Exploration*, Project Amazona. www.projectamazonas.com.

"Ritual Mortar," Orinoco Online. www.orinoco.org.

Clayton and Carole Robarchek, "Waorani: The Contexts of Violence and War," Waorani. http://webs.wichita.edu.

Elisabet Sahtouris, "Shuar," *Shuar, Life Web:* Shaur. www.ratical.org.

Michael S. Serrill, "Brazil: Something Terrible Happened," *Time International*, September 6, 1993, eLibrary. www.elibrary.com.

"Shuar Federation," Shuar Federation. www2.truman.edu.

Lawrence J. Speer, "Devastated by Peru's Shining Path," *Washington Times*, January 23, 1995, eLibrary. www.elibrary.com.

Sting, "Beginnings," The Rainforest Foundation UK. www.rainforest foundationuk.org.

Valerie Taliman, "Yanomami Massacre Had Longstanding History in Brazil," *Circle*, September 1, 1993, eLibrary. www.elibrary.com.

"Tribal Warfare and Blood Revenge," Tribal Warfare and Blood Revenge: History of the Shuar. www.head-hunter.com.

"Yanomami," *Orinoco Online*. www.orinoco.org.

"Yanomami Slaughtered for Gold," *Circle*, September 1, 1993, eLibrary. www.elibrary.com.

Index

Picture Credits

About the Author

Anne Wallace Sharp is the author of one book of adult nonfiction, *Gifts*, a compilation of stories about hospice patients; and several children's books, including *Daring Women Pirates* and six previous titles for Lucent Books. In addition, she has written numerous magazine articles for both the adult and children's market. A retired registered nurse, Sharp has a degree in history and a strong interest in indigenous cultures. Her other interests include reading, traveling, and spending time with her two grandchildren, Jacob and Nicole. Sharp lives in Beavercreek, Ohio.